A Day by Day Calendar
of Nova Scotia History

Leo J. Deveau

FORMAC PUBLISHING COMPANY LIMITED
HALIFAX

Copyright © 2017 by Leo J. Deveau

All rights reserved. No part of this book may be reproduced or transmitted in any form or by any means, electronic or mechanical, including photocopying, or by any information storage or retrieval system, without permission in writing from the publisher.

Formac Publishing Company Limited recognizes the support of the Province of Nova Scotia through the Department of Communities, Culture and Heritage. We are pleased to work in partnership with the Province of Nova Scotia to develop and promote our cultural resources for all Nova Scotians. We acknowledge the support of the Canada Council for the Arts, which last year invested $153 million to bring the arts to Canadians throughout the country. This project has been made possible in part by the Government of Canada.

Cover design: Tyler Cleroux

Library and Archives Canada Cataloguing in Publication

Deveau, Leo J., 1955-, author
    400 years in 365 days : a day by day calendar of Nova Scotia history / Leo J. Deveau.

ISBN 978-1-4595-0480-6 (hardcover)

    1. Nova Scotia--History--Miscellanea. I. Title.
II. Title: Four hundred years in three hundred sixty-five days.

FC2311.D48 2017   971.6002   C2017-903836-2

Formac Publishing Company Limited
5502 Atlantic Street
Halifax, Nova Scotia, Canada
B3H 1G4
www.formac.ca

Printed and bound in Canada.

CONTENTS

Introduction	4
Acknowledgements	6
JANUARY	8–29
FEBRUARY	30–47
MARCH	48–63
APRIL	64–83
MAY	84–99
JUNE	100–113
JULY	114–125
AUGUST	126–137
SEPTEMBER	138–149
OCTOBER	150–161
NOVEMBER	162–173
DECEMBER	174–185
Photo Credits	186
A Note on Sources	187
Index	188

More day by day Nova Scotia history at www.400years.ca

INTRODUCTION

The Port Royal Settlement, *by Francis Back.*

The Home Guard Platoon 7E, part of the Second World War Halifax Civil Emergency Corps, posed in front of the Gerrish Street Hall in Halifax in July 1943.

The idea for this book was inspired by an earlier work called the *Nova Scotia Book of Days*, authored and compiled by Shirley Elliott in 1979. Shirley wrote that her book was; ". . . an attempt to assemble a calendar of events which, in one way of another, relate to the day by day history of the Province of Nova Scotia." With 2017 being the 150th Anniversary of Confederation and Nova Scotia being one of the four provinces that signed the agreement to create a Canadian federation, I thought it was time to expand, broaden and update the effort that Shirley had undertaken. With her book as a template, I've endeavored to create a new work, which significantly reflects the many relevant historical narratives that encompass our province's rich social, cultural, political and economic realities.

Shirley's selective entries had a large political bent, reflecting many of the dominant British and Scottish narratives within our province's history. This was an understandable approach given the time in which she wrote as the Nova Scotia Legislative Librarian for the House of Assembly — a place which is steeped in so much of that unique history. Further, she wrote at a time that did not have desktop computers, the Internet or email. She drew from many primary and secondary print sources and though I too have reviewed similar sources, this new work has had the luxury of online access to similar sources through a multitude of databases, encyclopedias and archive holdings, and allowed me to communicate quickly with numerous contacts on clarifications and copyright clearances, including the identification and sourcing of permissions for many related images, illustrations and photos online.

Though many daily entries deal mostly with the domestic affairs of our province, there were also events that have taken place outside the province's borders that have impacted upon Nova Scotia and need to also be acknowledged. Consider, for example, in the twentieth century how the First World War unfolded in Europe, yet affected the people of Nova Scotia immensely — with 350,000 Canadian troops sailing from Halifax to an uncertain future. Thirty thousand Nova Scotian men volunteered to fight, and 3,400 didn't come home, leaving countless families and Nova Scotian communities to grieve their loss. And then there were the movements of thousands of people fleeing such conflicts, immigrating to our shores, seeking better lives and opportunities for their families. The Second World War and many other conflicts would repeat the scenario with more immigrants arriving, and more stories of loss, courage and resilience.

The movement of people to our Nova Scotian shores goes back centuries to when early explorers made their first contact with the Mi'kmaq people. The Mi'kmaq lived here within their ancient lands of Mi'kma'ki, going back thousands of years. And with the first European contact, there would soon follow various alliances and treaties, first with the French primarily at Port Royal and Louisbourg, then with the British, and eventually the province's colonial founding in 1749 under Governor Edward Cornwallis at Checbucto/British name; Chebouctou/French name, known in Mi'kmaq as K'jipuktuk.

Earlier, there had also been brief attempts by the Scottish, via Sir William Alexander (1602–1638) and the Royal Charter of 1621, to establish a colony in New Scotland (Nova Scotia means "New Scotland" in Latin) — first at Port de la Baleine in Cape Breton in 1629, and then later at Charles Fort/Port Royal. And though that settlement didn't last long, ending in 1632, that link continues to be present today in the Nova Scotia coat of arms and the flag of the province.

There were also the early Acadian settlements lasting almost 125 years (from the mid-1630s) and then their tragic deportation in 1755 — followed by their resilient return, only to find their fertile lands settled upon by the New England planters. Not long after, large numbers of Loyalist and former African slaves arrived, all fleeing the American War of Independence. And then eventually the arrival of the Highland Scots — they and many others would all settle in this province, participate in a system of government, seek democratic participation, create laws and conduct various enterprises.

Thus, like waves that rise and fall, our province's history encompasses a vast sea of events and peoples that moved toward the Nova Scotian shoreline, sometimes calm, and sometimes stormy, but always in motion, coming down to us through the generations, from a variety of locations, often interconnected in ways we only come to understand much later with hindsight.

It is also from Nova Scotia that the beginnings of democratic reform throughout the British Commonwealth began in what we now call Canada — first with

(TOP) El Jones.
(BOTTOM) Hank Snow.

400 YEARS IN 365 DAYS

Viola Desmond.

Natalie MacMaster.

representative government in Nova Scotia (1758) and then responsible government (1848). Prior to 1947, individuals born in Canada were classified as British subjects rather than Canadian citizens. The roots of Canadian democracy and citizenship began in Nova Scotia in 1758. Do all Nova Scotians know this?

Links to our province's past exist today in many ways, from flags to buildings, from street names in communities to regions, from food to festivals, now encompassing many of the world's cultures and religions. We also know that a province's history is more than just events. No longer do we see or understand our history solely as a single narrative, often with winners and losers, rather it encompasses a rich and diverse range of backgrounds, experiences, hopes and dreams.

This book reflects some of the extensive accounts that have come down to us through a range of overlapping historical records, from the writings of diarists and journal writers, to academic historians and genealogists. The variety of historical records that are now accessible is critically important in grasping the challenges and realities faced by all peoples that make up our province's history.

Such are the narratives of history. And utmost caution must be applied when interpreting such records from our comfortable armchair in 2017!

Like Shirley Elliott's *Nova Scotia Book of Days*, this book, I hope, will continue her legacy and commitment to deepen and broaden our understanding of the events and people that have shaped this province we know as Nova Scotia! It remains a selective compilation in that one couldn't possibly include everything. For example, I've left out many entries on the appointments of premiers and Lieutenant Governors, or lists of electoral outcomes, as all that information is now readily available online (on the Nova Scotia Legislative web site). Yet it is my sincere hope that this book captures a flavour of the diverse range of events that has created our province's people, our cultures and our rich heritage. The online site for this book includes many more entries than could be included in this edition (three times as many).

See www.400years.ca.

Acknowledgements

I've compiled this work in memory of the ten generations of my own family of Deveaus (paternal) and Gallants (maternal) that have lived both in Nova Scotia and Prince Edward Island since the mid-1600s, and from which I was born on PEI in 1955. Also for my daughters, Leah and Danielle, and their children Will, Ryan, George, Clay and Leo (all born in Nova Scotia), in the hope that they will come to know some of the many events and people that have shaped their province's history — and especially to take note of the roots of our democratic heritage and

Grand Pré National Historic Site.

the knowledge that citizenship begins first with a respect for all those who have come before us, and especially for those who have fought for our freedoms and paid the ultimate sacrifice — a sacrifice that demands from each of us a responsibility to participate in the civil life of our communities and our country, and most of all, to be informed — and when called upon, to vote!

This work is also written in memory of the late Jim Lotz, an immigrant to Canada from Liverpool, England, in the fifties, who inspired me with his writing discipline, constant curiosity, and sense of humour well into his mid-eighties. He taught me that if you want to change the music, "it's the organ-grinder you need to talk to — not the monkey!" And another Jim, the late Jim Snowdon, historian, educator and a dealer in antiques and art. His humor and curiosity in all things historical was an important example for me — to "pay attention, and be careful about assumptions and presumptions."

I also want to thank the many archivists and librarians across Nova Scotia, working in museums, special institutes, universities, colleges, and at the municipal, county and provincial levels, often working with very limited resources, who are keeping the important records of our provincial history in order and accessible as best as they can.

I wish to thank David McDonald, the current Nova Scotia Legislative Librarian, who assisted me in determining that the copyright for Shirley's book rested with the Speaker of the House of Assembly (currently the Honourable Kevin Murphy). And that upon my written request, and further discussions, I was given permission to use Shirley's material as a basis for this new work. The House of Assembly holds no responsibility for the accuracy of the content. That responsibility is solely mine. Formac Publishing had expressed interest in my efforts, and with some further reflection we decided upon the title for the book that you now have in your hands. I would like to sincerely thank Jim Lorimer, and his editorial and creative design team for their professional commitment, patience and encouragement.

To my partner, Coral, for her love, support and patience and for keeping my eyes on the goal of completing this book through various challenges and distractions for which many authors know all too well!

And finally, with gratitude to all those Nova Scotians who continue to value and respect all the facets of their province's history and wish to share it with all peoples.

JANUARY

January 1st

Construction was completed in 1819 on Admiralty House at Canadian Forces Base Stadacona, Halifax.

1819

The construction of Admiralty House was completed — a two-storey mansion set within the precincts of the Stadacona site of Canadian Forces Base Halifax. From 1819 to 1904, the building was the residence of the commander in chief of the Royal Navy's North American station. During the Second World War, it hosted regular convoy briefings. The building is an excellent example of British classicism in Canada. In 1979, it was recognized as a National Historic Site. It later became home of the Maritime Command Museum.

1823

Nova Scotia was the first province to issue coinage in penny and halfpenny tokens, appearing from 1823 to 1856. The thistle appeared on the reverse side to symbolize the link between old Scotland and new Scotland.

The Nova Scotia Thistle Penny, 1832.

1894

William D. Lovitt died in Yarmouth. Born in 1834, he was a prominent businessman who invested in over twenty-seven sailing vessels during his lifetime — one of Yarmouth's most active shipowners.

January 2nd

1878
The first meeting of the Royal Nova Scotia Historical Society was held. Dedicated to preserving and promoting the history of the province, over the years the society published a historical review, collections and a journal, which can be found at RNSHS.ca. Note their menu tab to "NS History Links."

1892
The name of the *Morning Herald* was changed to *Halifax Herald*. (Also see The first issue, January 14, 1875.)

Pat and Jim Lotz, 1993.

2015
James 'Jim' Robert Lotz, born in Liverpool, England, in 1929, died in Halifax. Lotz was an author, researcher and community economic development educator, and mentor to many aspiring writers in Atlantic Canada. His wife, Pat Lotz, born in Brighton, England, in 1930, was an author, librarian and editor, and died in 2012.

January 3rd

A scene of children skiing by Maud Lewis.

1863
The Earl of Mulgrave declared the skating rink on Park Street open — first covered rink in Canada. Throughout Nova Scotia, residents always enjoyed winter outings, as these later paintings by Maud Lewis indicate. (Also see During the winter, January 16, 1838.)

January 3rd (cont'd)

Joseph Howe, publisher of the Novascotian.

1828
The first weekly issue of the *Novascotian* under Joseph Howe was published. A year earlier, Howe had been joint owner with James Spike of the *Weekly Chronicle* newspaper, which later changed its name to the *Acadian*. But by December 1827, at the age of twenty-eight, Howe relinquished his share in the *Acadian* and purchased the *Novascotian* from George Young. A month later, he married Catherine Susan Ann (née McNab) and they went on to publish the *Novascotian*. (Also see McNab, July 5, 1890.)

Soon after beginning the paper, Howe travelled extensively throughout Nova Scotia and published his impressions in *Western Rambles* (1828); *Eastern Rambles* (1829–1831); and *Letters from the Interior* (1832). By 1839, there were thirteen newspapers being published in Nova Scotia — nine in Halifax, one in Yarmouth, two in Pictou and one in Lunenburg.

Moses Coady (1882–1959): "When you stop pioneering, you die."

1882
Moses Coady was born in the Margaree Valley of Cape Breton (d. 1959). He became a Roman Catholic priest and a visionary adult educator. He was best known for his leadership role in the Antigonish Cooperative Movement that began in 1929 in response to the chronic decline in the fisheries, the closing of mines and the onset of the Great Depression. In 1939, Coady published his classic work, *Masters of Their Own Destiny*. He dedicated the book, "To all those unnamed noble souls who without remuneration are working overtime in the cause of humanity." He died in 1959.

1892
Anselme Chiasson was born in Cheticamp (d. 2004). He became a noted Roman Catholic priest, educator and writer, who made significant contributions to the documentation of Acadian history and folklore (authoring in 1942, with Daniel Bourdreau, the eleven volumes of *Chanson d'Acadie*). He was named to the Ordre des francophones d'Amérique in 1979, a chevalier in the French National Order of Merit in 1999, a chevalier in the Order of La Pléiade in 2002 and made an officer in the Order of Canada in 2003.

JANUARY 4ᵀᴴ

Church of Saint Paul and the Parade of Halifax in Nova Scotia, 1777 by John Fougeron.

1760
St. Paul's Church, Halifax, was incorporated. Established by royal decree by King George II. Construction of the church had begun in 1750 and was completed by 1763.

St. Paul's Church.

January 5th

The Cabot Trail in winter.

2004
The Cabot Trail was named one of the top six scenic drives in North America by the *Michelin North America 2004 Road Atlas*.

1588
The earliest approximate map of the geographical area that later became known as Nova Scotia (but was at the time a part of the Mi'kmaq land, referred to as Mi'kma'ki) was created by Portuguese cartographer Diogo Homem (1521–1576). He had been banished from Portugal in 1545, but later settled in Venice where he made the map in Latin. It was later translated to English for the High Court of the British Admiralty. John Cabot's earlier map of 1544 was not as detailed as Homem's.

The earliest approximate map of Nova Scotia, created by Portuguese cartographer Diogo Homem (1521–1576).

January 5th (cont'd)

Parliamentary Poet Laureate George Elliott Clarke.

2015
African Nova Scotian poet, playwright and educator, George Elliott Clarke (b. 1960), was appointed Canadian parliamentary poet laureate. A native of Windsor, and a seventh-generation Canadian of African-American and Mi'kmaq heritage, Clarke became an officer of the Order of Nova Scotia and the Order of Canada. He has received the Governor General's Literary Award for Poetry (2001), the National Magazine Awards' Gold Medal for Poetry and the Dr. Martin Luther King Jr. Achievement Award.

January 6th

1972
CBC affiliate in Sydney, CJCB, aired the CBC documentary *The Vanishing Cape Breton Fiddler*. Produced by Ron MacInnis, it informed Cape Bretoners about a complacency that had set in about how traditional music with the Cape Breton fiddle was facing a possible extinction. By June, the Cape Breton Fiddlers' Association had been formed, and during the summer of 1972 over two hundred fiddlers were identified on Cape Breton. A Festival of Cape Breton Scottish Fiddling was planned for July 6–8 1973.

2015
Ngena (Gena) Bernard died suddenly of a heart attack at age thirty-six. She left behind four children and a life full of promise. She was a full-time student at Dalhousie University, was planning a career in social work, and a graduate of Dalhousie's Transitional Year Program where she received the Jonathan Skeete Award. The Ngena Bernard Memorial Transition Year Program bursary has been established to assist African Canadian single parents who are graduates of the Dalhousie University Transition Year Program and who plan to study social work.

January 7th

1936
Arthur R. Richardson, carpenter, farmer, harbour pilot and politician, died in South Bar (b. 1862). He was president of the Independent Labour Party in 1918. In the July 27, 1920, provincial election, Richardson won a seat in Cape Breton County and was part of the official opposition through a period of difficult labour relations. He stepped down in 1925.

January 8th

1977

The idea of a Nova Scotia Youth Orchestra germinated in Bridgewater, where Robert Raines was conducting the South Shore Concert Orchestra. Raines had some students assisting in the orchestra, and that was when the thought arose that Nova Scotia should have a provincial youth orchestra. Frances Power became a co-founder and Robert Raines became the first Nova Scotia Youth Orchestra conductor. Forty years later the orchestra was described by renowned professional conductors and musicians as one of the finest youth orchestras in Canada.

January 9th

1877

The Academy of Music in Halifax officially opened on Pleasant (later Barrington) Street.

1893

The school of Horticulture opened in Wolfville.

The Academy of Music in Halifax (on the location that became home to the Maritime Centre on Barrington Street, with the St. Matthew's Church spire in the background).

January 10th

1866
Daniel Cobb Harvey was born on PEI (d. 1965). An archivist and public educator, he was considered one of the most significant twentieth-century historians of the Maritime Provinces. He was the Nova Scotia provincial archivist from 1931 to 1956. He was the author of *Heart of Howe* (1939), *The Intellectual Awakening of Nova Scotia* (1933), *The Age of Faith in Nova Scotia* (1946) and a number of other important works and numerous articles.

1987
Judge Raymond Bartlett was removed from the bench of the Nova Scotia Family Court after a provincial Judicial Council investigation into his frequent speeches which berated women in court.

1965
The *Micmac News* began publishing. Developed by Roy Gould in Membertou, it was published until 1991 by the Union of Nova Scotia Indians and the Native Communications Society of Nova Scotia. The Beaton Institute at Cape Breton University has digitized the complete issues online at: BeatonInstitute.com. See their menu tab "Micmac News 1965–1991."

January 11th

1832
The Halifax Mechanic's Institute opened with a speech by Joseph Howe. He warned his audience that in inaugurating the institute, their first steps might be ". . . assailed by the sneer of the ignorant and the ridicule of the idle." The first president of the institute was Dr. William Grigor, with Howe as vice-president.

1890
The first Canadian Pacific Railway telegraph office opened in Halifax. The following year, the CPR completed a telegraph line from Truro to Halifax. The line was built along the Intercolonial Railway line.

January 12th

1836
The African School was established in Halifax from the Protestant Gospel School (Bray School), and was soon followed by similar schools at Preston, Hammonds Plains and Beech Hill.

1956
Sam Langford, prizefighter, died in Boston (b. 1883 in Weymouth Falls). In 1999, Langford was voted Nova Scotia's top male athlete of the twentieth century. Jack Dempsey once said of Langford, "I think Sam Langford was the greatest fighter we ever had." African Nova Scotian playwright Jacob Sampson later wrote a play about Sam Langford's life called *Chasing Champions*, which went on to win six Theatre Nova Scotia Merritt Awards, including Outstanding Actor, New Play and Production.

Sam Langford.

January 13th

1814
The Royal Acadian School opened on Argyle Street in Halifax. Established by British officer and reformer Walter Bromley (1775–1838), schooling was offered for middle-income students as well as low-income women, black students and immigrants. Bromley also gave public exposure to the poor living conditions of the Mi'kmaq, encouraging material improvement and education. The school also welcomed Protestants and Catholics. The school was controversial, but had the support of leading individuals such as Thomas McCulloch. One of its students would be Joseph Howe. By 1816, there were four hundred students enrolled. Bromley left the province in 1825, but the school had played a key role in promoting free education and later inspired Howe's push for educational reforms.

1885
Alfred Fuller, founder of Fuller Brush Company, was born in Welsford, Kings County. Fuller Brush became a successful early twentieth-century US company.

January 14th

Miners' bodies being recovered from the McGregor Mine after the explosion of January 14, 1952. A large crowd, including draegermen, can be seen around a stretcher.

1875
The first issue of the *Morning Herald*, later the *Halifax-Herald*, was published. (Also see *Morning Herald*, January 2, 1892.)

1851
Joseph Howe paid a second visit to England as an agent of the government of Nova Scotia, on behalf of the Intercolonial Railway project, to negotiate with the Colonial Office for financing support. His broader effort was to appeal directly to the people of England to colonize the British North American provinces. He concluded his speech at Southampton on this day. (Also see John Howe, December 28, 1780.)

1952
An explosion occurred in McGregor Mine, Pictou County. Twenty-two men were working 1,400 feet underground for the Acadia Coal Company. Nineteen men died.

1980
The Vietnamese Association of Nova Scotia (VietNS) was founded as a result of the first waves of Vietnamese immigrants who arrived in Nova Scotia after the fall of Saigon in 1975. More than thirty years later, the association constituted not only the original "boat people" but also extended family members and immigrants from other provinces who have chosen the Maritimes as their home. (Also see The last of United States troops, March 29, 1973.)

January 15th

The Nova Scotia Mass Choir, in front of the Africville Museum (Church), June, 2016.

1992
The newly formed, thirty-five member, multicultural Nova Scotia Mass Choir, under the direction of Scott MacMillian, performed their first *Tribute to Martin Luther King Jr.* concert in collaboration with Symphony Nova Scotia. Their repertoire of black gospel music went on to raise awareness of some of the cultural contributions of African Nova Scotians to the fabric of Nova Scotia. (Also see The Civil Emergency Corps, January 24, 2015.)

1792
A fleet of fifteen ships left Nova Scotia for Sierra Leone — with Thomas Peters, a former slave, black soldier and leader (1738–1792); Methodist ministers Boston King (the blind preacher) and Moses 'Daddy' Wilkson; Baptist preacher David George; and Cato Perkins and a group (1,196) of Black Loyalists. This represented over half the population of Birchtown. David George recorded, "The White people in Nova Scotia were very unwilling that we should go." He later recalled, "though they had been very cruel to us, and treated many of us as bad as though we had been slaves." The fleet was an initiative of Lieutenant John Clarkson, a British abolitionist and a founder and first governor of Sierra Leone for formerly enslaved African-Americans.

JANUARY 16TH

Jimmy, Raylene, Heather, Cookie and John Morris. The Rankin Family.

2000

John Morris Rankin, of Judique, Cape Breton, died at the age of forty. He was a member of the much-loved Rankin Family musical group from Mabou, Cape Breton Island. Coming from a family of twelve siblings, John Morris and his brother Jimmy and sisters Cookie, Raylene and Heather released their first independent cassettes in 1989 *(The Rankin Family)* and 1990 *(Fare Thee Well Love)*. Both featured traditional jigs and reels, original songs and Celtic folk songs. They went on to record under Capitol Records, EMI, Liberty and MapleMusic, winning many Canadian music awards along the way, including a 1992 Juno Award nomination for Most Promising New Group of the Year.

January 16th (cont'd)

1838
During the winter, residents around Halifax participated in various recreational activities. On the political scene, it was during this time that the old Legislative Council was dissolved and reconstituted. In its place an Executive Council and a Legislative Council were established. (See also, After a vote... February 2, 1848.)

"Coasting" at Halifax, *by James Fox Bland, 1859.*

1865
The Morning Journal changed to *Unionist and Halifax Journal.*

1906
After 157 years of British military presence in Halifax, Canadian forces took over from the British, behind them came the Royal Canadian Regiment, the Royal Canadian Garrison Artillery, and the Royal Canadian Engineers.

January 17th

1948
Allister MacGillivray was born in Glace Bay. He became a noted songwriter, now best known for his music composition *Song of the Mira* — "I'll trade you ten of your cities for Marion Bridge / And the pleasure it brings" — written in the early 1970s. Also well known as a guitarist (formerly with Ryan's Fancy), a folklorist, author and record producer. His work, considered largely Celtic in style with a Maritime flavour, has been played by countless groups and many individual artists. He published *The Nova Scotia Song Collection* in 1989 and in 1991, *Diamonds in the Rough: 25 Years with The Men of the Deeps.* In 2013 he was inducted into the Order of Canada.

1920
The United States enacted the *National Prohibition Act* — known formally as the *Volstead Act* — banning the production, importation, transportation and sale of alcoholic beverages, which lasted till December 1933. This began an elaborate system of smuggling, known as "rum-running", carried out by entrepreneurial Nova Scotia fishermen and ship owners to supply thirsty Americans with rum from the West Indies and brandy and whisky from St. Pierre and Miquelon. The following year (1921) rum runners would also supply thirsty Nova Scotians. For over ten years a game of "cops and robbers" evolved between smugglers, bootleggers and moonshiners and officials from Customs, the Department of Revenue and temperance inspectors. (Also see Clifford Rose, March 7, 1889; The rumrunner *I'm Alone,* March 22, 1929.)

January 18th

1878
Alexander Graham Bell demonstrated his telephone to Queen Victoria at Osborne House. Two years earlier on March 10, 1876, Bell had uttered the famous words to his assistant, "Mr. Watson, come here, I want you," which are considered to be the first ever spoken on a telephone. Later, on August 3, 1876, Bell held further tests and made the first intelligible telephone call from building to building. Bell would later transfer the Canadian patent rights to his father, Alexander Melville Bell (1819–1905), who established the Bell Telephone Company of Canada in 1880 and began the first telephone networks in Canada. Alexander Graham Bell would later say, "Of this you may be sure, the telephone was invented in Canada. It was made in the United States."

Alexander Graham Bell (1847–1922).

2014
Bob Stead, mayor of Wolfville for fifteen years, died. A former employee of Acadia University (and 1964 graduate), he was elected to the Wolfville Town Council in 1988. He became recognized for his health-related vision and leadership. In 2015, the Union of Nova Scotia Municipalities presented Stead with the Ken Simpson Memorial Award for outstanding public service and leadership in Nova Scotia municipal government.

1821
Halifax Harbour froze over.

January 19th

1799
James Boyle Uniacke (d. 1858) was born, son of Richard John Uniacke and Martha Maria Delesdernier. He was the first premier of Nova Scotia (1848–1854) to lead the first responsible government in Canada, while also serving concurrently as the colony's attorney-general. Joseph Howe, his provincial secretary, would join him in creating new democratic reforms. A full list of Nova Scotia premiers can be reviewed at: NSLegislature.ca on the History menu tab. (Also see Richard John Uniacke, November 22, 1753.)

January 19th (cont'd)

1915

Anna Harriette Leonowens (née Edwards) died in Montreal (b. 1831 in India). For nearly two decades (1878–1897), she lived in Halifax with her daughter Avis and son-in-law, Thomas Fyshe, who was general manager of the Bank of Nova Scotia. She had been a governess and tutor to the King of Siam's sixty-seven children and wrote an autobiography of her experience called *The English Governess at the Siamese Court* (1870). She was an active supporter of the arts, education and literature in Halifax. She left Halifax in 1897, but her name and memory live on in an art gallery, the Anna Leonowens Gallery, connected to the art school she began (first as the Victoria School of Art and Design), later known as the Nova Scotia College of Art and Design.

Anna Leonowens (1831–1915).

1929

The Coat of Arms of the Province of Nova Scotia was readopted by Royal Warrant — the oldest provincial achievement of arms in Canada, and the oldest British coat of arms outside Great Britain. They fell out of use when Nova Scotia joined the Confederation in 1867.

The Coat of Arms of Nova Scotia.

1863

The Nova Scotian Institute of Natural Science met for the first time.

January 20th

1976

The College of Cape Breton Press (later Cape Breton University Press) began publishing operations. It closed down in 2016.

1971

The Dominion Atlantic Railway Bridge across the Avon River at Windsor was blown up following the causeway completion.

January 21st

1842

Joseph Howe hosted the notable author Charles Dickens on his first visit to Canada, attending the opening of the twentieth Nova Scotia Legislature. Dickens had already published *The Pickwick Papers* (1837) and would later publish *A Christmas Carol*. (Also see Christmas classic, December 19, 1843.)

2008

Former chief of Pictou Landing, Raymond Francis died. He was known for starting the movement to resolve the environmental problems resulting from pollution in the Boat Harbour area of Pictou County. (Also see Pictou Landing Native Women's Group, September 28, 2012.)

January 22nd

The Halifax Club.

1862
The Halifax Club was established on Hollis Street in Halifax. It became a social gathering place for a number of the city's bankers, politicians and influential businessmen, who met there on a regular basis.

JANUARY 22ND (CONT'D)

(TOP) The Canadian Museum of Immigration at Pier 21. (BOTTOM) Children evacuated from Britain during the Second World War arrived at Pier 21 in Halifax.

2009
Halifax's Pier 21 became Canada's newest national museum — the Canadian Museum of Immigration at Pier 21, dedicated to the recognition and celebration of immigrants' and new Canadians' contributions to this country's cultural history and heritage. The Pier 21 site had opened as an immigrant centre on March 8, 1928, processing over 1.5 million immigrants coming to Canada, including over 64,446 war brides and their children between 1942 and 1948 alone, as well as 3,000 British evacuee children and hundreds of thousands of refugees. Pier 21, along with the Ocean Terminals, was also the departure point for 494,000 Canadian servicemen and women heading to Europe during the Second World War. It closed on March 28, 1971. (Also see Ruth Miriam Goldbloom, August 29, 2012.)

January 23rd

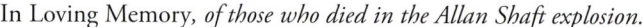

In Loving Memory, *of those who died in the Allan Shaft explosion.*

The Honourable Justice Catherine Benton.

1918
The Town of Stellarton mourned the loss of eighty-eight men in the Allan Shaft mine explosion. The mine was considered one of the world's most dangerous collieries. Fifty years earlier, one hundred miners had also died at this seam of coal.

2017
Catherine Benton was appointed by the Nova Scotian government as a new judge to the provincial judiciary — she was the first Mi'kmaw woman to be appointed to such a position.

January 24th

1940
Harry Piers died (b. 1870). A librarian, curator, naturalist, historian, artist, editor and author, his family roots went back to the establishment of the Halifax settlement in 1749. By 1899, Piers was the deputy keeper of public records and helped complete in 1911 the cataloguing of Thomas Beamish Akins's early historical settleme nt records. In 1927 he authored a biography of Nova Scotia portrait-painter Robert Field, entitled *Robert Field, Portrait Painter in Oils, Miniature and Water-Colours and Engraver.*

In 1931, Piers became the curator of the Provincial Museum and the librarian for the Provincial Science Library. As a natural historian, he did extensive inventories in botany and geology, and later in anthropology with the collections of Mi'kmaq artifacts and in the oral and written accounts of such Mi'kmaq elders as Jerry Lonecloud. He was also active in the Royal Nova Scotia Historical Society.

JANUARY 24TH (CONT'D)

The Home Guard Platoon 7E, part of the Second World War Halifax Civil Emergency Corps, posed in front of the Gerrish Street Hall in Halifax in July 1943.

2015

The Civil Emergency Corps, more commonly known as the Home Guard, was honoured in the Nova Scotia Mass Choir's annual tribute, *Dr. Martin Luther King Jr., The Dream Continues*, at the Rebecca Cohn Auditorium. The Home Guard was a civilian defence force formed during the Second World War to provide police, fire, health and various other services when necessary. Home Guard Platoon 7E was made up entirely of African Nova Scotian men and women who provided service support in north-end Halifax. (Also See The newly formed Nova Scotia Mass Choir, January 15, 1992.)

1999

George Elroy Boyd's play *Consecrated Ground* ended its production run at the Eastern Front Theatre. The play depicted the consequences to a black family of the razing of Africville in the 1960s and the relocation of its 400 residents to more "progressive" public housing. It was nominated in 2000 for a Governor General's Award in Drama and published in an anthology of contemporary African Canadian drama.

January 25th

Wallace R. MacAskill (1887–1956), NS photographer extraordinaire.

1956

Wallace R. MacAskill died. He was born in St. Peter's, Cape Breton, in 1887. A prominent marine photographer (trained in New York in 1907), he moved to Halifax in 1915 and later opened his own business in 1929. He published *Out of Halifax* (1937) and *Lure of the Sea* (1951), and was a recipient of numerous international awards for his photographic achievements. A collection of over 4,599 of his images is online at the Nova Scotia Archives.

Alden Nowlan, one of Canada's most popular twentieth-century poets.

1933

Alden Nowlan was born in Stanley, Nova Scotia (d. 1983). He became recognized as one of Canada's most popular twentieth-century poets. Also a journalist, dramatist and novelist, he once stated that ". . . if it hadn't been for the Windsor public library, I might have ended up just working in the woods." (By the age of sixteen he often hitchhiked to the library, where he began his lifelong passion for learning and reading.) For Nowlan, poetry was ". . . all about people, and to hell with literature." He first published works of poetry in 1958 and by 1967, when his collection *Bread, Wine and Salt* was published by Clarke Irwin, he was regarded as one of the most original voices of his generation, and received the Governor General's Award for English Poetry.

January 26th

2013
Daurene Elaine Lewis, died (b. 1943). She was an educator, the first black mayor in Canada — Annapolis Royal in 1984 — and the first black woman in Nova Scotia to run in a provincial election. She was a direct descendant of Rose Fortune, a black Loyalist who arrived in Annapolis Royal in 1784.

2000
The Nova Scotia Museum of Natural History opened the travelling exhibit *Remembering Black Loyalists, Black Communities* for the start of African Heritage Month.

January 27th

1896
The Royal Hotel in Wolfville was badly damaged by a fire, but was later rebuilt and "furnished with all the modern conveniences of electric light, bells, hot and cold bath." By 1927, its name was changed to the Evangeline Inn, costing four dollars for a room, or twenty-five dollars per week. By the 1940s, the inn was leased by Acadia University to serve as a men's residence for men returning from the war. In the summer of 1960, the inn was torn down and replaced by an Irving service station. The station was later removed and a town-clock park opened on the property.

January 28th

Schooner Bluenose, 1959, *by Jack L. Gray.*

1946
The famous schooner *Bluenose* was lost off Haiti. The ship was abandoned on a reef, with no loss of life.

January 29th

1831
A public meeting was held in Halifax to promote temperance, namely the prohibition of the sale or use of alcohol.

January 30th

1965
The state funeral service for Winston Leonard Spencer-Churchill took place at St. Paul's Cathedral in London, England. He had died on January 24. His funeral witnessed one of the largest assemblages of states-people the world had ever gathered for such a service. Later, his coffin was taken up the River Thames and to the funeral train at Waterloo station for a journey to the family plot at St. Martin's Church at Bladon, near Churchill's birthplace at Blenheim Palace. On January 20, 1980, a statue of Churchill was unveiled outside the former Spring Garden Memorial Library in Halifax.

The statue of Winston Churchill outside the former Spring Garden Memorial Library by sculptor Oscar Nemon — based on a photograph of Churchill when he visited Halifax in 1943.

January 30th (cont'd)

Fortress Louisbourg.

Fort Anne, Annapolis Royal.

1920
Fortress Louisbourg was designated a National Historic Site of Canada by the Historic Sites and Monuments Board of Canada (HSMBC). Named the largest reconstructed eighteenth-century French fortified town in North America (and maybe the world), between 1713 and 1758 it was a place of profound significance in the great French-British struggle for empire. Fort Anne at Annapolis Royal was also been designated by the HSMBC on this date as a National Historic Site (fortified since 1629). It was the first (and oldest) site acquired by the federal government for national historic purposes that has subsequently remained under Parks Canada administration. The British withdrew the garrison from Annapolis Royal in 1854.

1860
The Victoria Rifles, one of the oldest black soldier regiments to be established in Canada, was established in the wake of the Crimean War (and on the eve of the American Civil War).

1838
Legislative Council was opened to public and reporters. The council at this time was unelected.

January 31st

1854
Conservative James W. Johnston (1792–1873) introduced a bill in the Nova Scotia Legislature for the "Union of the Colonies." He felt this was the best way for Nova Scotia to resist being absorbed into the United States, but he found no support for the bill. His sentiments were ahead of his time by thirteen years. He would become premier from 1857 to 1860 and 1863 to 1864.

1951
The main building at Mount Saint Vincent University was destroyed by fire.

FEBRUARY

February 1st

A Dominion Coal Company colliery in Reserve Mines, Nova Scotia, about 1900.

1893
The Dominion Coal Company was incorporated by American businessman and promoter Henry M. Whitney, with the first steel produced on December 31, 1901 — beginning over one hundred years of boom and bust cycles for the Sydney steel plant. The Sydney area grew from 2,427 in 1891 to 17,728 by 1911. The company went through various corporate restructures, ultimately being taken over by the Government of Nova Scotia through the Sydney Steel Corp. on November 22, 1967. It was closed in 2001. (Also see Black Friday, October 13, 1967.)

February 2nd

A scene from Evangeline *(1913–1914).*

1914
In 1913, Canada's first feature film, *Evangeline*, was produced, based on Henry Wadsworth Longfellow's poem of the same name. It was premiered in Halifax on this date in 1914. Produced by the Halifax-based Canadian Bioscope Company, the film is now considered lost.

February 2nd (cont'd)

The Mellis family from Syria on the cover of The Coast.

2016

On this date, Syrian refugee Dana Mellis commented on her experience of having to leave her country, "They were shouting, 'Leave the city or you will die.' We had to leave immediately, so we very quickly found some clothing and some important papers . . . and then we left."

She became a scholarship student and plans to study pharmacy at Dalhousie University. The Mellis family arrived from Syria in Nova Scotia on January 12, 2016. They were five of "roughly 1,000 government-sponsored refugees who landed in the province in 2016."

1848

After a vote of twenty-eight to twenty-one, the old Nova Scotia Executive Council resigned and a new Council was appointed representing the Reformers (later to be known as Liberals) — with James Boyle Uniacke as the first premier of the province (with Joseph Howe as provincial secretary). Responsible government became a reality in Nova Scotia.

February 3rd

1939

Four hundred and twenty-one volunteer soldiers from the Mackenzie-Papineau Battalion began to disembark at Halifax (February 3 to 18). Of the 1,300 who had left to fight fascism in the Spanish Civil War (1936–1939), half had been killed. Nineteen volunteers were from Nova Scotia. Joining the battalion was illegal at the time, so there was no official welcome for the returning men. But on October 20, 2001, Governor General Michaëlle Jean dedicated a monument to the battalion in Ottawa.

2017

About 150 people of different faiths formed a support circle around Halifax's largest mosque (the Ummah Mosque) as a public gesture to show solidarity with the city's Muslims after the fatal shooting at a mosque in Quebec City on January 29 that left six people dead.

February 3rd (cont'd)

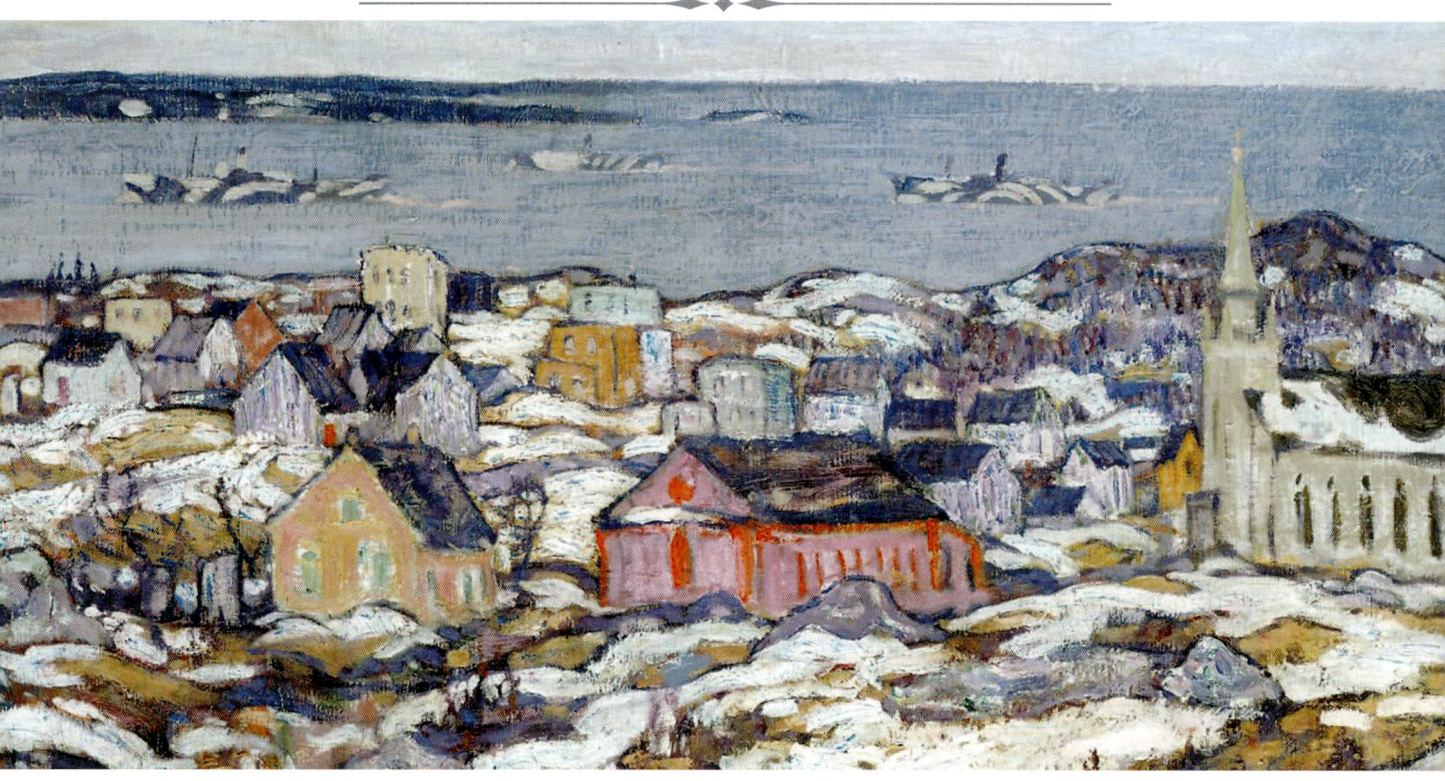

Entrance to Halifax Harbour, *1919, by A.Y. Jackson.*

1919
Returned war artist and member of the Group of Seven, A.Y. Jackson visited fellow artist and friend Arthur Lismer in Halifax to paint the final stages of soldiers returning to peace in Canada. One of the pieces he created during this time was *Entrance to Halifax Harbour*. This painting was later acquired by the Tate Gallery in England.

1970
The 11,379-ton Liberian oil tanker *Arrow* went aground at Cerebus Rock in Chedabucto Bay, five miles from Arichat. Bunker oil escaped to pollute over 125 miles of shoreline.

February 4th

1992
Tom Paul, Mi'kmaq spiritual leader, poet and activist from Eskasoni, Cape Breton, died of a heart attack, at age forty-nine. He was a veteran of protests at Wounded Knee, South Dakota, and Restigouche, Quebec, among other places, and was awaiting trial in connection with the seventy-eight-day armed standoff at Oka in the summer of 1990.

1980
The Cape Breton–based rock group the Minglewood Band was nominated for a Juno Award for Most Promising Group of the Year.

February 5th

1920
Main building at King's College, Windsor, destroyed by fire.

February 6th

1918

The Representation of the People Act (known also as the Fourth Reform Act) was passed in the United Kingdom. It was designed to reform the electoral system to include all men over twenty-one who could vote in the constituency where they were resident. And to include women over thirty years old if they were a member of a Local Government Register, or were married to a member, were a property owner or voting in a university constituency. Nova Scotia women were granted this right later that year. (Also see The Nova Scotia Franchise Act, April 26, 1918).

February 7th

1965

Viola Desmond died in New York City while on a visit, aged 50. She was buried at the Camp Hill Cemetery in Halifax. She was born Viola Irene Desmond Davis in Halifax in 1914. She was a 32-year-old black Nova Scotian businesswoman when, on November 8, 1946, she challenged racial segregation at a film theatre in New Glasgow, Nova Scotia. She refused to leave a 'whites only' area of the Roseland Theatre and was unjustly jailed for twelve hours and convicted of a minor tax violation used to enforce segregation. (Also see Carrie Best, July 24, 2001.) Desmond's case later went to the Nova Scotia Supreme Court and helped start the modern civil rights movement in Canada. Nova Scotia's segregation laws were dismantled in 1954. Her actions occurred nine years before the famed incident by civil-rights activist Rosa Parks, with whom Desmond is often compared. She was granted a posthumous pardon by the NS government, the first to be granted in Canada, by the Honourable Mayann Francis, the lieutenant governor of Nova Scotia at the time. The story of Viola Desmond had largely been forgotten till Nova Scotian journalist Sherri Borden Colley brought Desmond's story to readers in March 2010.

Viola Desmond, c. 1935.

1908

An explosion in a Port Hood, Cape Breton, mine killed ten miners, four of whom were residents of the area, and six were Bulgarian. The mine was later flooded from the sea. A list of over 2,584 names of miners who have died in various mining accidents in Nova Scotia (and where) are listed in the "Men in the Mines" NS Archives database, found at Archives.NovaScotia.ca at the Mining topic tab.

February 8th

1950

The Cunard liner S.S. *Samaria* arrived in Nova Scotia with 1,556 passengers at Pier 21. Jim Spatz was one of those passengers. He was less than a year old, travelling with his parents, Simon and Riva, who were Holocaust survivors. Spatz would go on to a successful medical practice in Montreal. Later he would return to Halifax to join his father in his property management and development business called Southwest Properties. He was one of over a million immigrants who landed at Pier 21 between 1921 and 1971.

Halifax businessman Jim Spatz.

1961

Gladys (Richardson) Porter (1893–1967) was the first woman to be elected to Nova Scotia Legislature, taking her seat for the Progressive Conservatives in the Kings North riding. She had served previously as mayor of Kentville from 1946 to 1950, and from 1954 to 1960. She was an MLA till her death on April 30, 1967.

1956

The Liberal government (under Premier Henry Hicks) announced its intention to grant recognition to unions of workers at public boards and commissions. This did not include the largest group of provincial employees — the civil service. However, with government assurance, by April an association of Nova Scotia civil service workers began to take shape. And by December 5, 1957, the newly elected Conservative government cabinet, under Premier Robert Stanfield, approved the establishment of the Nova Scotia Civil Service Association. Through various changes, civil service employees are now organized under the Nova Scotia Government and General Employees Union (NSGEU), representing over 31,000 public and private sector employees. (Also see NSGEU, April 18, 1958.)

Between 1981 and 2010, the total public service employment at the federal, provincial and local levels in Nova Scotia represented a 28.3 per cent share of total employment in the province.

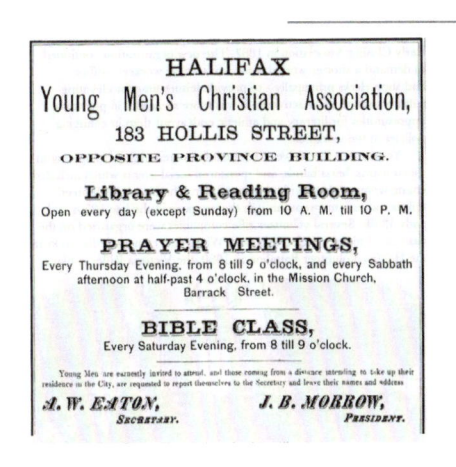

February 9th

The YMCA one of Halifax's Christian-related temperance groups.

1848
Mayflower Division, Sons of Temperance, organized in Halifax, as well as other Christian related groups to support temperance values. (Also see Public Meeting, January 29, 1831.)

1756
At Fortress Louisbourg, the trial of Pierre LeRoy and Anne Lando took place, and both were accused of murdering Lando's husband. They were both found guilty and sentenced to death. LeRoy was executed that summer, strangled and broken on the wheel. Lando was hung and burned, with her ashes thrown to the wind. That same summer, a number of French soldiers who had deserted were captured. All were executed by hanging.

February 10th

1924
Max Ferguson was born in Britain (d. 2013). He came with his family at the age of three to London, Ontario. He started in radio broadcasting after graduating from the University of Western Ontario. He arrived at CBC Radio Halifax in 1947, where he began a popular radio show called *Rawhide*, featuring a wonderfully eccentric and caustic old curmudgeon introducing various pieces of "cowboy" music. The show was moved to Toronto in 1949, but he was able to move it back to Halifax in the mid-fifties. The show continued till 1962. He later hosted *The Max Ferguson Show*, which continued for many years. In the words of veteran broadcaster Michael Enright, Ferguson was "the CBC's first major radio star." Max Ferguson retired to Cape Breton in 1998 after a fifty-two year radio broadcasting career.

Max Ferguson gained notoriety portraying different characters on the CBC Radio show Rawhide, *which featured country music.*

1937
The French Acadian newspaper *Le Petit Courrier* was first published. It was founded by Désiré d'Eon as a one-page broadsheet of local-interest news for French readers in southwest Nova Scotia. D'Eon later moved the paper's operations to West Pubnico. With ownership changes in 1970–71, the paper was renamed *Le Petit Courrier de la Nouvelle-Écosse*, becoming a newspaper that reflected daily Acadian life across the province. In October 1977, the paper was named *Le Courrier*.

1885
A serious accident occurred at Vale Colliery, Pictou County. Thirteen men were killed by an explosion of gas. On May 3, 1883, seven men had died in an accident when a drawbar broke on a slope trolley.

February 11th

1747
The Battle of Grand Pré took place at 3 a.m. in a blinding snowstorm. A detachment of British troops from Massachusetts under Colonel Arthur Noble and troops from Annapolis totalling five hundred men, were all being billeted in the houses of Acadian inhabitants in the Grand Pré area when they were attacked by French troops from Quebec under the command of Captain Coulon de Villiers, accompanied by Acadian Militia and Mi'kmaq warrior forces estimated to also number about five hundred men. A ceasefire was later called and terms agreed to. Acadian reports indicated that both parties buried 120 men after the attack, while many were wounded or taken prisoner.

1834
African Nova Scotians from the communities north of Halifax, Dartmouth, Preston, Eastern Passage, Chezzetcook and others submitted a petition to the government asking to receive representation in the House of Assembly. Abolition of slavery by the British government took place in 1834.

February 12th

1813
Maria Frances Ann Morris was born (d. 1875). She became an art teacher and Nova Scotia's first native-born professional woman artist, and also the first native-born botanical artist in Canada. She had been encouraged by botanist Titus Smith and supported by local patrons, publishing a series of lithographs, representing over 146 Nova Scotia wildflower species in 1840, 1853 and 1866. A collection of her paintings was also shown at the universal exposition in Paris in 1867.

2001
Halifax's Salter Street Films, Atlantic Canada's biggest television and film production company, was sold to Alliance-Atlantic Entertainment of Toronto for $80 million. Founded in 1983 by Michael and Paul Donovan, it was responsible for producing such comedy shows as *This Hour Has 22 Minutes, Made in Canada, Blackfly*, the sci-fi series *LEXX* and a number of feature films. It also produced Michael Moore's Best Documentary Oscar-winning *Bowling for Columbine* (2002).

Actoea Alba & Rubra, Red and White Baneberry, 1840, by Maria Morris.

FEBRUARY 13TH

Fishermen's monument at Peggy's Cove, by William Edward deGarthe.

1983

William deGarthe died (b. 1907). He was a Finnish-born painter and sculptor who lived much of his life in Peggy's Cove. He trained under Stanley Royle at Mount Allison University, and at other art schools in New York and Paris. After his arrival back in Nova Scotia in the early forties, he taught commercial art at NSCAD. He later created many works of art that went on to national and international exhibits and became popular amongst individual and corporate collectors. He also became known for his sculpture at Peggy's Cove dedicated to "Nova Scotia Fishermen." Inspired by the sight of the statue of Christ the Redeemer in Rio de Janeiro, the project was 80 per cent completed when deGarthe died in Toronto while undergoing cancer treatment. The sculpture was bequeathed to the Province of Nova Scotia where it can be viewed in Peggy's Cove.

1896

The first electric streetcar started a test service in Halifax. The service became fully operational on May 31. (Also see the Halifax Street Railway Company, June 11, 1866.)

The Halifax Electric Tramway Company open summer car no. 11, in Halifax, 1897.

February 14th

1997
The Mi'kmaq Kina'matnewey, representing twelve member communities across Nova Scotia, signed a historic educational jurisdiction agreement with the government of Canada, which transferred control of Mi'kmaq education to the Mi'kmaq people.

1883
William Roy Mackenzie was born in River John, Pictou County (d. 1957). Educated at Dalhousie and Harvard, he became a literary scholar, writer and folksong collector. Considered the father of ballad collecting in Canada, he was the first scholar to collect Anglo-Canadian and Nova Scotian songs. Mackenzie's work and further publications, such as *Ballads and Sea Songs from Nova Scotia* (1928), provided inspiration to Helen Creighton and other collectors. His papers were eventually collected at the Dalhousie University Archives.

February 15th

1979
Springhill-born Anne Murray (b. 1945) received her Grammy Award in absentia in Los Angeles — the first solo Canadian female artist to reach number one on US charts and to achieve a gold record in the United States (*Snowbird,* in 1970). She has sold more than 55 million records, earning thirty-one Junos. She is a Companion of the Order of Canada, and a recipient of the Order of Nova Scotia (2002). (Also see *Singalong Jubilee,* July 3, 1961.)

1880
The first quintuplets in Canada were born in Little Egypt, Pictou County. The parents were Mr. and Mrs. Adam Murray. The quintuplets made their family a total of twelve. Unfortunately, all of the quintuplet babies died within a few days. As reported in the *Winnipeg Times* on March 1, 1880, P.T. Barnum wanted to mummify the babies and take them on tour.

Anne Murray.

February 16th

Winston 'Scotty' Fitzgerald.

1914

Winston 'Scotty' Fitzgerald was born at White Point, Victoria County, Cape Breton (d. 1987). He became a renowned Cape Breton fiddler and a pioneer in recorded performances of music, which influenced later generations of players. He began playing at the age of eight and, while working in the shipyards in Halifax during the 1930s, he played with Hank Snow. (Also see Hank Snow, May 9, 1914.) As a veteran of the Second World War, he settled in Sydney, formed a group and recorded numerous 78s and LPs. His popularity grew further when he was featured as a member of the Cape Breton Symphony Fiddlers (formed in 1974, beginning with Wilfred Gillis, Jerry Holland, Bobby Brown, Tom Szcyesniak, Peter Magadini, Fitzgerald and John Allan Cameron), which played on *The John Allan Cameron Show* — first on CTV Montreal, and later moved to CBC Halifax (1979–1981). (Also see John Allan Cameron, November. 22, 2006.)

1967

The Canadian Royal Commission on the Status of Women commences its work. Broadcaster, journalist and senator Florence Bird (1908–1998) was chosen as the commission's chair. Over the next three years, the commission called for submissions from organizations and individuals. It received approximately 500 briefs, 1,000 letters of opinion and also held a series of public hearings across the country. The work of the Commission was considered by many to be groundbreaking and resulted directly in significant improvements to the lives of many Canadian women and, as a result, to Canadian society as a whole.

2012

It was announced that Brigadier General (Retired) John James Grant was appointed the thirty-second lieutenant governor of Nova Scotia (2012-2017). Following him, on June 14, 2017, the Honourable Arthur Joseph LeBlanc was appointed the thirty-third lieutenant governor of Nova Scotia.

1929

The Strand Theatre opened in New Waterford, with seating for 650 individuals to view movies.

February 17th

1820
The Halifax Poor Man's Friend Society was founded in Halifax by a local group of business and professional men who aimed to ". . . relieve the wants of the numerous poor, and destroy the system of public begging." Society members regularly visited the poor to examine their state of need and offer assistance in the form of money, food, supplies or employment. By 1822, money was discontinued as a standard form of relief. In 1823, the society opened a soup kitchen to meet the increased demand for relief. Faced with public criticism and declining funds, the society disbanded on February 16, 1827.

February 18th

1901
Death of William Johnston Almon (b. 1816 in Halifax), physician and senator. He was the first doctor in North America to use chloroform as an anaesthetic.

February 19th

1895
The first Jewish synagogue in Nova Scotia was dedicated in the former First Congregation Baptist Church on the corner of Starr Street and Hurds Lane, in Halifax. Generous contributions were made by Christian congregations in the city, and repairs were made so the building could serve as a synagogue and a school for the community. The first wedding was witnessed there within an hour of the synagogue dedication — between Sarah Cohen and Harry Glube. Jews had been arriving in Halifax since the early 1750s, and more arrived in the 1780s. A hundred years later, many immigrated to Nova Scotia from the pogroms in Russia, settling in Yarmouth, Sydney and Halifax. The Halifax Jewish community grew to be the largest east of Montreal. The Congregation Sons of Israel synagogue in Glace Bay began in 1901.

Nova Scotia's first Jewish synagogue in a former Baptist church on Starr Street, Halifax, 1895.

1849
Joseph Howe spoke in the Nova Scotia House of Assembly, expressing the importance of having a superintendent of schools, school libraries, adequate compensation for teachers and free schools.

1921
The first permanent dial telephone exchange in Nova Scotia began operating in North End Halifax.

FEBRUARY 20TH

1823
Halifax Harbour was frozen over below George's Island at 13 degrees below zero. The harbour froze over on other occasions, as this illustration indicates in 1859, with the arrival of Cunard's RMS *America*.

A moment frozen in time. Samuel Cunard's steamship RMS America *arrives in Halifax, Valentine's Day, 1859. Signed 'Avery.' From* The Marine Curator, *March 8, 2013.*

FEBRUARY 21ST

1753
As part of the conflict triggered by the British decision to establish a new presence on mainland Nova Scotia a group of Mi'kmaq captured a British vessel with a crew of four along the Eastern Shore (referred to as the Attack at Mocodome — later known as Country Harbour, NS). The four were taken captive — John Connor, James Grace, Michael Haggarthy and John Power. The latter two were killed and Connor and Grace were held captive. They later escaped after killing six Mi'kmaq (including a woman and child). In response, the Mi'kmaq, led by Jean-Baptiste Cope, retaliated by luring a Halifax trading ship to the Jeddore area where they overpowered and killed seven of the eight crew members. The eighth member, Anthony Casteel, was held for ransom and eventually freed at Port Toulouse.

February 21st (cont'd)

1849
The first Nova Scotia Pony Express began operations. Carrying news, the express departed Halifax about 5 p.m. on Wednesday, headed to Amherst, and arrived in Saint John about 8 p.m. on Thursday — travelling time, Halifax to Saint John, about 27 hours. The service was run by Daniel Craig and Hiram Hyde, who had organized a fast horse courier service then called the Halifax Express, later known as the Nova Scotia Pony Express. Their express also connected with a chartered steamship service across the Bay of Fundy. The weekly service only ran till November 1849, when it ended due to the completion of the telegraph line that connected Halifax with Saint John, Boston and New York. There was also a brief express service to Victoria Beach, through Kentville, but it ended on October 2.

1891
The Springhill mine explosion occurred with 125 men killed — seventeen of them were boys sixteen years of age and younger. Many more were injured.

Illustration from Story of the Springhill Colliery Explosion: Comprising a Full and Authentic Account of the Great Coal Mining Explosion at Springhill Mines, Nova Scotia, February 21st, 1891, *by R.A.H. Morrow.*

February 22nd

2017
The Nova Scotia Government announced their "Culture Action Plan" to create a culture innovation fund worth $1.5 million and provide $2 million a year to the creative industry fund. Critics of the plan felt that it failed to provide new resources and did not restore the Nova Scotia's film tax credit.

February 23rd

1970
The "Encounter on Urban Environment" conference was held in Halifax. The National Film Board made a film about the event — ". . . held by a panel of specialists from different fields who met with members of this urban community to consider the future of the area and the responsibility of the citizens and government in planning the future."

February 23rd (cont'd)

J.A.D. McCurdy piloting the Silver Dart *over Baddeck Bay — the first airplane flight in Canada, 23 February 1909.*

1909
The first controlled flight in the British Empire in a heavier-than-air machine, called the *Silver Dart*, took place in Baddeck. The airplane was flown by Douglas McCurdy, who had worked with Alexander Graham Bell's Aerial Experiment Association when they had designed the machine. He flew it off the ice of Bras d'Or Lake.

February 24th

Ashley MacIsaac at the Burlington Sound of Music festival, 2010.

1975
Ashley MacIsaac was born in Creignish, Cape Breton. He became a well known fiddler, singer and songwriter, receiving three Juno Awards and creating fourteen albums. He later published an autobiography, *Fiddling with Disaster* (2003). He made many tours, produced loved music and collaborated with many artists.

February 24th (cont'd)

The Africville Museum Church.

Aerial view of Africville.

2010

Halifax Regional Municipality Mayor Peter Kelly apologized to the people of Africville on behalf of City Council for the destruction of their community nearly forty years before, mainly between 1964 and 1967. The last resident in Africville left in 1970. The apology included the allocation of some land, the restoration of the Africville name (changing from Seaview Park back to Africville) and $3 million for the construction of a replica of the Seaview United Baptist church that had stood at the geographic and emotional heart of Africville till 1967 (established in 1849 as the Campbell Road Baptist Church), which now houses the Africville Museum. For many years, the people of Africville had worked to achieve a settlement. Africville was named a National Historic Site in 2002. The apology also included the establishment of the Africville Heritage Trust that would carry out the work for the design and building of the museum.

February 24th (cont'd)

1816
Charles Inglis, the first Colonial Bishop in the British Empire, died in Aylesford. He was later buried under the chancel at St. Paul's Church.

Charles Inglis (1734–1816), by Robert Field.

2015
A French salute was given with glasses of the newly issued Fortress Rum at the former military garrison at Louisbourg — the first rum to be matured onsite in almost three hundred years, being sold in traditional bottles, sealed with wax, capturing the authentic spirit of New France's historic rum trade. The rum was produced by Authentic Seacoast Distilling Company in partnership with Parks Canada and the Fortress of Louisbourg association. Mitch McNutt, general manager of the Association, stated that, "Rum is a very important part of the story of the Fortress of Louisbourg, being a New World drink and a popular drink in the 18th century."

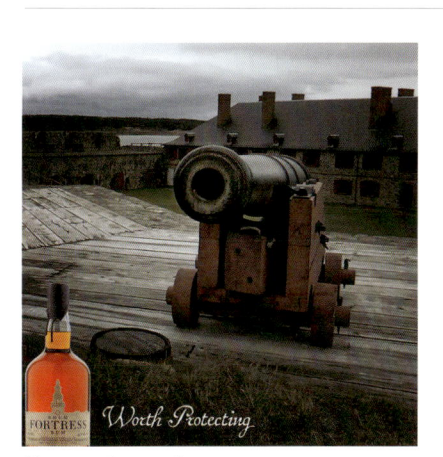

Fortress Rum advertisement.

FEBRUARY 25ᵀᴴ

2013
The Halifax Women's History Society (HWHS) was founded. Its mission was to research and make known the untold story of the remarkable contributions that women have made to the history of Halifax. "A Woman on the Waterfront" was the Society's first project — to erect a monument to honour women volunteers during the Second World War, provide public acknowledgement of their numerous contributions and educate the citizens of the day and the future about the essential services that women willingly and generously provided. On March 9, 2017, the monument design was announced. The piece was called "*The Volunteers/ Les Bénévoles*" by artist Marlene Hilton Moore.

2017
The African Nova Scotian Music Association (ANSMA) Awards were hosted at the Spatz Theatre in Halifax (formed in 1997).

A Woman on the Waterfront promotional graphic.

FEBRUARY 26ᵀᴴ

1958
Clarissa (Clara) Archibald Dennis died. Born in Truro on November 24, 1881, she was educated at Mount Allison and Dalhousie. The daughter of Senator William Dennis, she became a reporter and noted photographer and author on Nova Scotia history and Mi'kmaq culture and personalities. She produced over 3,000 photographs, including many that featured the Mi'kmaq culture. (Also see Agnes Dennis, April 21, 1947.)

1789
The Halifax garrison's new Grand Theatre, located near the central waterfront, opened on this day with a production of *The Merchant of Venice*.

1610
Jean de Biencourt de Poutrincourt (1557–1615) sailed from Dieppe, France, for Acadia (Port Royal settlement) with his son, Charles de Biencourt (1592–1624). Poutrincourt had made his first voyage to Acadia in 1604 with Pierre Dugua de Mons (and Samuel de Champlain). He was appointed governor of Port Royal in 1606 by de Mons. The British attacked and destroyed Port Royal in 1613 and Poutrincourt returned to France. (Also see Samuel de Champlain, May 16, 1604.)

February 27th

1939
The art-deco styled Vogue Theatre opened in downtown Sydney, Nova Scotia, heralded as the "newest type of theatre" with "modernity as its keynote." It would close in 1998 and be demolished in April 2008.

1799
Sir Edward Belcher, sailor and author, was born in Halifax (d. in London, 1877). The great-grandson of Governor Jonathan Belcher, he led the last and largest Admiralty Arctic expedition (five ships) in an unsuccessful attempt to rescue the Franklin Expedition.

February 28th

1952
Vincent Massey was sworn in as the new governor general of Canada — the first Canadian-born person to be appointed to the position. The Massey lectures were named in his honour.

Vincent Massey, Governor General of Canada (1952–1959).

400 YEARS IN 365 DAYS

MARCH

March 1st

1840
Alexander MacLean Sinclair was born in Glen Bard, Antigonish County. He became a Presbyterian minister, author, educator and Gaelic scholar. While he served as a minister in the community of Belfast, Prince Edward Island (1888–1906), he self-published several books on indigenous Gaelic culture in Nova Scotia filled with song, lore and culture. He later retired back to Nova Scotia, where he lectured on Gaelic language and culture at St. Francis Xavier and Dalhousie universities. One of his students, Angus L. Macdonald, later became premier of Nova Scotia.

1977
Prime Minister John George Diefenbaker addressed the Nova Scotia House of Assembly.

March 2nd

1939
The Queen Hotel fire on Hollis Street claimed twenty-eight lives and injured many more. The hotel had been built in sections between 1849 and 1908. There were no alarm or sprinkler systems.

The Queen Hotel fire.

March 2nd (cont'd)

The Nova Scotia Legislative Library, formerly the Supreme Court Chambers for Nova Scotia — the site of the trial of Joseph Howe.

1835

The trial of Joseph Howe (age thirty-one) was held in the Nova Scotia Supreme Court Chambers (later, the NS Legislative Library). Writing about the incompetence and self-interested graft happening among local political elites, he was charged with seditious libel. The six-and-a-quarter-hour trial witnessed Howe as he represented himself before a jury, and cited case after case of civic corruption. Judge Brenton Halliburton presided. He instructed the jury to find Howe guilty, but the jurors thought otherwise and found Howe innocent. In part of his defence Howe stated, "Yes, gentlemen, come what will, while I live, Nova Scotia shall have the blessing of an open and unshackled press. But you will not put me to such straits as these, you will send me home to the bosom of my family, with my conduct sanctioned and approved; your verdict will engraft upon our soil those invaluable principles that are our best security and defence." When Howe was declared innocent, his case was seen as the first to establish the fundamental basis for the freedom of the press in Nova Scotia and later in Canada.

March 3rd

1815
Peace between United States and Great Britain was proclaimed in Halifax.

1841
St. Mary's College was incorporated by an Act of Legislature. It would later become Saint Mary's University.

March 4th

1885
The Nile Voyageurs returned to Halifax on the *Hanoverian*. The Voyageurs had participated in the Nile Expedition to the Sudan to rescue British-Egyptian garrisons cut off by a Muslim uprising led by the Mahdi. The Voyageurs numbered 386 men and officers, of whom 374 returned.

March 5th

1930
The mace, gift of Chief Justice Robert E. Harris and Mrs. Harris, was used for the first time in the Nova Scotia Legislature. An ancient symbol of royal authority, it was delegated in Nova Scotia to the House of Assembly under the responsibility of the Speaker of the House. The power of the Crown is represented in the ceremonial mace, and when the House is in session, the mace, the Speaker's authority to conduct the business of the House, is always present on the clerk's table. It is in the care of the sergeant-at-arms.

The mace on the clerk's table in the Nova Scotia Legislative Chamber.

1915
Henry D. Hicks was born in Bridgetown in the Annapolis Valley (d. 1990). He served as premier from 1954 to 1956. He was first elected as a Liberal from Annapolis County in 1945, and was later defeated by Robert Stanfield's Progressive Conservatives. He became president of Dalhousie University in 1963, serving till 1980.

March 6th

1947

The gypsum freighter *Novadoc*, sailing from Deep Brook, Annapolis County, for Staten Island, New York, was lost at sea. The last message heard from the ship was a distress call at 2:17 a.m. on March 3, that reported they were foundering in heavy seas about twenty-five miles off Portland, Maine, with their hatches and bulkhead badly damaged. After a prolonged search, no trace of the ship or her twenty-four crew was ever found (including thirteen Nova Scotians). In July of 2005, a monument was erected on the Digby waterfront to honour the crew who perished on the *Novadoc*.

(TOP LEFT) The *Novadoc* was lost at sea.
(TOP) July 2005, unveiling of a monument to honour the crew who perished on the *Novadoc*.

March 7th

1956

The Nova Scotia tartan was registered at the Court of the Lord Lyon. "The Nova Scotia Tartan was the first provincial tartan in Canada. It reflects the profound contribution of the Scots to the founding of Nova Scotia, and the pioneer settlement of the old Royal Province. The very name Nova Scotia resounds with early Scottish colonial ambition; in Jacobean Latin it meant New Scotland. Being one among many large groups of settlers in the 18th and 19th centuries, the Scots brought with them the powerful lore of the Highlands. From this, the folk art revival of the present century brought forth Nova Scotia's recent emblem. Originally designed by Bessie Murray in 1953 for the agricultural exhibition in Truro, the popular tartan was adopted . . . in 1955 through an Order in Council." (Nova Scotia Legislature)

The Nova Scotia tartan.

1889

Clifford Rose was born. He became a self-educated carpenter, but by 1925 he was appointed the municipal temperance inspector for the town of New Glasgow. He wrote a diary of his reflections and the manuscript is considered a valuable historical document on the prohibition period in Canada and Nova Scotia. But not all his writings were about chasing the "demon rum." Writing on October 9, 1927, about one of his trips, "Had a beautiful drive today through West River valley and back past the famous Church at Gairloch. It is a noble institution — newly painted. The Ku-Klux-Klan met there last Thursday night for church service. What Scottish memories and stories could be told around that famous old Church . . . " Copies of the complete texts of his writings are available at the libraries of Saint Francis Xavier University and the University of New Brunswick.

March 8th

2013

Billy Downey died (b. 1934). He was employed for forty years as a porter/conductor for the Canadian National Railway/Via Rail. He was also the well-known owner (with brother, Graham) of the Arrows Night Club in Halifax — known as "the soul centre of the Maritimes," and for breaking down the barriers of segregation and providing a venue for world-class performers to play in the city from 1962 to 1979. The club opened first on Creighton Street, moving later to Agricola, then to Brunswick Street. Performers such as Sam Cooke, Ike and Tina Turner and Miriam Makeba performed at the Arrows, as well many local musicians.

1991

Nina Cohen (née Fried) died in Toronto (b. Glace Bay, March 17, 1907). She was a well-known community activist from Glace Bay who "dedicated herself to many social reform and cultural causes throughout the province from the 1930s–70s." She was also a founding member of the Miners' Folk Society in 1964 (with sixty charter members), and the Cape Breton Miner's Museum, ". . . in the face of considerable skepticism." She received the Canadian Red Cross Medal of Merit, and Woman of the Century 1867–1967 for the province of Nova Scotia and for the National Council of Jewish Women. Nina Cohen once said, "The Cape Breton miner is no ordinary man. His story has a heartbeat; it should not be allowed to die." (Also see Cape Breton Miners' Museum: July 31, 1967.)

March 9th

1997

Montreal-born jazz pianist Joe Sealy won a Juno award for his CD of original music, *Africville Suite* (1996). It includes twelve pieces reflecting on places and activities in Africville, where Sealy's father was born. Sealy was working and living in Halifax during the time of the destruction of Africville, and began the suite in memory of his father.

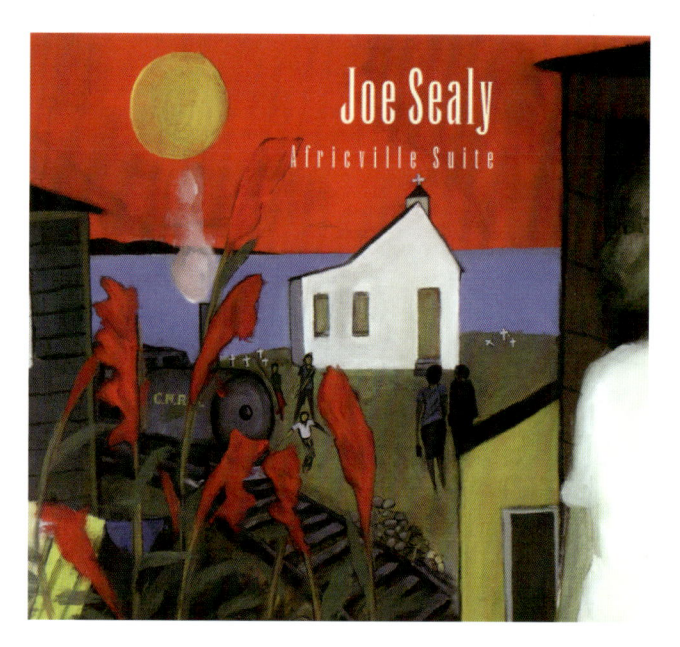

(LEFT) *Joe Sealy.*
(RIGHT) *Album cover.*

March 10th

Bellevue House (centre).

1885

Bellevue House, residence of British military commanders on Spring Garden Road, was destroyed by fire. The land on which it stood was originally purchased in 1800 by the Duke of Kent, who had commanded the British forces in North America from Halifax. Built in 1801, it was described as an "almost palatial residence." It also hosted members of the royal family during visits to the colony. After Bellevue House burned down it was rebuilt. Its replacement was demolished in 1955. It then became the location of the new Halifax Central Library.

Bellevue House was constructed in 1801. It was the residence of the commander-in-chief of the British military (1801–1906).

March 11th

Island in the Ice, *1987, by Tom Forrestall.*

1936
Artist Tom Forrestall was born in Middleton. He studied art at Mount Allison University under Lawren Harris and Alex Colville, and devoted himself to painting. He would later be considered one of the leading figures in visual arts in the Maritimes, having exhibited extensively throughout the region and in prominent galleries worldwide.

March 12th

2013
Halifax-based filmmaker, writer and director William D. MacGillivray (b. 1946) won a Governor General's Award in Visual and Media Arts for his forty years of filmmaking. MacGillivray won a Gemini Award for Best Motion Picture in 1988 for his film *Life Classes*. It was also Canada's official selection in competition for the Golden Bear at the Berlin Film Festival of 1988 (Norman Jewison's *Moonstruck* won that year). He produced five other feature films, and wrote and directed a thirteen-part comedic television series (*Gullages* for the CBC Network), ten short films and seven documentaries. On his work, MacGillivray commented, "You never know what other people will think about your work. You do the work you do and some people like it and some people don't. I've tried to tell stories that mean something to us in Atlantic Canada."

William (Bill) MacGillivray.

March 12th (cont'd)

1876

James Platino Johnston (also referred to as James R. Johnston) was born in Halifax (d. March 3, 1915). He became the first black Nova Scotian to graduate from university (Dalhousie), in 1898, and was called to the bar as a lawyer on July 18, 1900, becoming the third black lawyer in Canada. Johnston became a criminal defence counsel and activist, being involved in the African United Baptist Association (AUBA) and other community organizations. He was also a member of the Conservative Party, which had been instrumental in repealing the school segregation laws in Nova Scotia. He strongly advocated for an industrial school for black children.

Graduation portrait of James Platino Johnston, 1900 by Notman Studio.

March 13th

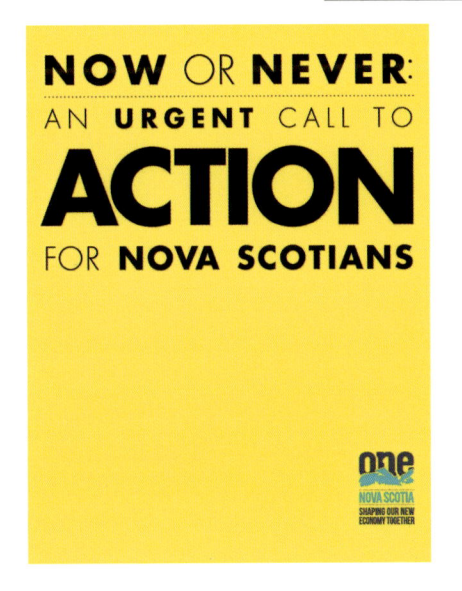

2017

The OneNS Measurement Collective officially launched their OneNS Dashboard to provide key online Nova Scotia–based economic and demographic indicators that reflect progress toward "the nineteen Ivany Goals," which were released in *The Report of the Nova Scotia Commission on Building Our New Economy*.

1828

The *Novascotian* noted the existence of a Society for the Diffusion of General Knowledge in Spanish Town, Jamaica, and the membership there of a Halifax-educated African Nova Scotian, Cuffy Montagu James, who had been educated at Preston (Nova Scotia), "having mastered the alphabet and the rudiments of psalmody."

OneNS Measurement Collective Poster.

March 14th

The Steam Ferry Mic Mac by Dusan Kadlec.

2017

Eric MacNearney died in Halifax (b. 1930). A well-known businessman and entrepreneur, he was a founding partner in the development of the Halifax Historic Properties, and later the establishment of Truefoam. He was an avid sports enthusiast and voracious reader in all things historical. He wrote in his introduction to *Inspired Halifax, The Art of Dusan Kadlec* (Nimbus, 2003), "Very few vestiges remain of nineteenth-century life in Halifax and other seaports, but one can relive the past while enjoying the work of the artist, as he captures for the feeling of both urgency and tranquility that was part of life in those times."

1840

A duel between Joseph Howe (age thirty-six) and John Halliburton (age thirty-nine) occurred in Point Pleasant Park, near the Martello Tower. Halliburton missed with his shot and Howe fired into the air. The duel was the result of "bitterness spawned by the drive for political reform." Mr. Halliburton was also the Clerk of the Executive Council and son of the chief justice, Sir Brenton Halliburton, who had presided over Howe's trial in 1835.

John C. Halliburton.

March 15th

1932
Mi'kmaw poet and songwriter Rita Joe was born in Whycocomagh (d. March 20, 2007). She was referred to as the poet laureate of the Mi'kmaq people. In 1978, her first book of poems, *The Poems of Rita Joe*, was published. She published six more books and was made a Member of the Order of Canada in 1989, and of the Queen's Privy Council for Canada in 1992.

1952
HMCS *Haida* was recommissioned in Halifax — the first Canadian warship under the new reign of the Queen Elizabeth II.

March 16th

1872
Sara Corning was born in Chegoggin, Yarmouth County. Corning trained as a nurse in the United States and joined the American Red Cross during the First World War. In December 1917, she was amongst the first to volunteer to tend the sick and suffering after the Halifax Explosion. In 1921, working for a relief agency, she arrived in a small village at the foot of Mount Ararat in what became Turkey to take charge of an orphanage. In 1922, as fighting and lawlessness escalated, Corning became a central figure in the evacuation of the port city of Smyrna (and saved thousands of children's lives). After the rescue, she helped establish an orphanage in Greece for the stateless orphans. She was summoned to Athens in June 1923, where King George II of Greece awarded her, and others involved in the rescue mission, the Silver Cross Medal of the Order of the Saviour. Sara worked at the orphanage until 1924, when she returned to Turkey to work in a residential training school until 1930 when the Near East relief effort was disbanded. Upon retirement, she returned to Chegoggin.

Sara Corning, c. 1900.

March 17th

2010
The Hockey Hall of Fame installs the puck Sydney Crosby used to score the winning goal in overtime (3–2 Canada over US) at the Vancouver Olympics final game.

400 YEARS IN 365 DAYS

March 18th

1819
The Lottery Bill passed for raising £9,000 to erect a bridge over the Avon River in Windsor.

March 19th

1920
The Annapolis Royal Post Office, seen here before and after the fire of 1920. Built in 1890, it was designed by Thomas Fuller, chief Dominion architect. Fuller had designed over 140 structures, including the Parliamentary Library and the Halifax Armoury. (Also See After three years, December 31, 1898.)

(TOP) Annapolis Royal Post Office after fire, March 19, 1920.
(RIGHT) Annapolis Royal Post Office, c. 1900.

1750
The frame of the first hospital in the new British settlement at Chebucto/Halifax was constructed (on the site which later became the Government House). By 1752, forty-nine patients were recorded.

1842
The Province of Nova Scotia passed an act to provide for the "Instruction and Permanent Settlement of Indians." Joseph Howe was appointed Indian Agent.

March 20th

1804
Lieutenant Governor John Wentworth (1737–1820) received orders to seize all Spanish vessels entering Halifax Harbour. Wentworth was the first civilian governor appointed in Nova Scotia, serving from 1792 to 1808. (See also, Sir John Wentworth, April 8, 1820.)

March 21st

2006
The African Diaspora Association of the Maritimes was formally incorporated with a goal to ensure that people of African descent who lived in the Maritimes had access to opportunities for cultural, social, political and economic engagement.

1904
An earthquake was felt in New England, New Brunswick and Nova Scotia.

March 22nd

2017
The Cape Breton Liberation Army returned in a new stage musical at the Highland Arts Theatre in Sydney (March 22–30). Inspired by Paul MacKnnion's *Old Trout Funnies*, writer and theatre artistic director Wesley Colford wrote *The Return of the Cape Breton Liberation Army*, set in 2017. The sixteen-person cast featured singing, dancing and brawling.

The rum-runner I'm Alone.

1929
The rum-runner *I'm Alone* was sunk in the Gulf of Mexico. Registered out of Lunenburg, she was intercepted by the coast guard off Louisiana, returning from Belize with liquor. She disobeyed orders to stop and was shelled and sunk. Seven crew members were rescued and one died. The captain, John 'Jack' Randell, was arrested and jailed in New Orleans. The incident drew international attention.

March 23rd

1752
The *Halifax Gazette* was published by John Bushell (1715–1761) — the first newspaper in Canada. Bushell arrived in Halifax from Boston in early 1752 to take over a small printing establishment begun by a former Boston partner, Bartholomew Green Jr., who had died shortly after arriving in Halifax. Bushell was a printer first, and lacked newspaper experience. But by 1758, Anthony Henry (1734–1800), a veteran fifer of the British forces at the capture of Louisbourg, took up residency in Halifax and became Bushell's partner. He assumed control of the paper after Bushell's death in 1761.

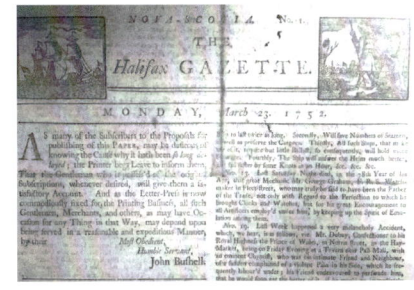

The Halifax Gazette, *March 23, 1752.*

MARCH 24TH

1998
Yvonne Atwell became the first African Nova Scotian woman to be elected as an MLA (for the NDP). Born in East Preston, she later wrote, "Social activism is about building a place where no matter what this person does in their life, they'll never forget what they learned. It's not like they took some type of training and then left halfway through it — even then, it's not a failure, because it's the lessons that you learned to get where you need to go."

MARCH 25TH

1943
Radio station CJFX broadcast for the first time from Antigonish. The station was subsequently owned and operated by the Atlantic Broadcasting Co., and branded as 98.9 X-FM.

MARCH 26TH

Don Messer and His Islanders.

1973
Don Messer died in Halifax (b. 1909). He was leader of Don Messer and His Islanders, an old-time music group — the most popular in Canada during the mid-twentieth century. They had formed in 1939 for CFCY radio in Charlottetown and in the '50s appeared regularly on CBC-TV Halifax. Eventually they had a national broadcast show, winning a wide audience. When the show was cancelled in 1969 it brought many complaints from viewers and raised questions in the House of Commons. *Singalong Jubilee* (see July 3, 1961) replaced *Don Messer's Jubilee*. (Also see Anne Murray, February 15, 1979.)

March 26th (cont'd)

1921

The *Bluenose* schooner was launched at Lunenburg. Designed by William J. Roué, it was intended for both fishing and racing. It sailed under the command of Captain Angus Walters during the 1920s and 1930s. (Also see Angus Walters, August 11, 1968; Bluenose, October 26, 1938.) The vessel became a provincial icon for Nova Scotia. While hauling freight near Haiti, the schooner hit a reef and sank in 1946. A replica of the ship, *Bluenose II*, was launched in 1963. (Also see Bluenose II, July 24, 1963.)

Launch of the Bluenose.

1751

In a conflict prompted by the British move to expand their presence on mainland NS without advance dialogue with the Mi'kmaq treaty partners, the Dartmouth settlement was attacked by Mi'kmaq warriors on three occasions. On March 26, fifteen persons were killed, seven wounded and six were taken prisoner. A further attack on May 13, reported twenty killed. In June another attack occurred, with eight killed and fourteen taken prisoner.

March 27th

1945

Annie Mae Aquash (Pictou) was born in Indian Brook (Mi'kmaq name Naguset Eask). She later moved to Boston and became involved in the American Indian Movement in the Wounded Knee incident. She disappeared in late 1975, and her body was found in February 1976 on a desolate road near the Pine Ridge Indian Reservation in South Dakota. The cause of her death was covered up, but later evidence and charges came forward. Three men within the American Indian Movement had raped and murdered her with an execution-style gunshot. She had been falsely accused of being an FBI informant. In 2002, Mi'kmaw filmmaker Catherine Martin produced a film about Annie Mae, called *The Spirit of Annie Mae*, where, among others, she featured Annie Mae's two daughters. Daughter Denise Maloney commented in the Truro *Daily News* that "Indians tried to paint my mother's murder as some sinister, 'Big Government' conspiracy, when in fact it had nothing to do with that. She was killed by her own people." (January 6, 2011).

March 28th

1966

Ben Christmas, long-time chief at the Membertou Reserve died (b. 1896). A devout Roman Catholic, he was a highly respected prayer and choir leader. He became chief of his community in 1919 at the age of twenty-three. For a short time he was also president of the North American Indian Brotherhood.

1940

A pilot boat collided with a Newfoundland vessel and sank in the Halifax Harbour, with the loss of nine lives.

March 29th

1867
Queen Victoria gave Royal Assent to the *British North American Act* (*BNA Act* — "An Act for the Union of Canada, Nova Scotia, and New Brunswick, and the Government thereof; and for Purposes connected therewith"). The *Act* comprised a major part of the Constitution of Canada, and entailed the original creation of a federal dominion and established the framework for much of the operations and structure of the Government of Canada. The *BNA Act* was renamed the *Constitution Act, 1867*, when it was patriated to Canada in 1982. July 1, celebrated as Canada Day, is the anniversary of the *Act*'s entry into force on July 1, 1867. (Also see, The Charlottetown Conference... September 1, 1864.)

1973
The last United States troops left Vietnam on this day. A peace agreement had been signed in Paris in January, 1973, between the Viet Cong, North and South Vietnam, but fighting continued till the North Vietnamese Army captured Saigon in April, 1975. Some estimates state between 30,000 and 40,000 American war resisters, commonly called draft dodgers, came to Canada between 1971 and 1972. Many settled in Nova Scotia.

March 30th

1776
As a result of the American War of Independence (also known as the American Revolution, 1775–1783), the British had to evacuate Boston and set sail for Halifax. General Howe's army began to arrive in Halifax on this day from Boston with 11,000 troops and 1,100 civilians. More arrived on April 1. By 1782–83, 25,000 to 30,000 Loyalists would arrive in Nova Scotia, almost doubling the colony's population. Over half would move to settle in what became the province of New Brunswick, as well as the colony of Cape Breton. Two-thirds of the people in Nova Scotia at this time were of Yankee birth or parentage.

Part of the Town and Harbour of Halifax in Nova Scotia, Looking Down Prince Street to the Opposite Shore, 1777, by Dominic Serres after Richard Short.

2012
Premier Darrell Dexter revealed the Nova Scotia government committed up to $304 million in loans as part of Irving Shipbuilding's successful bid for the $25 billion federal combat vessel shipbuilding program.

1832
Bank of Nova Scotia began operations as a chartered public bank (intended to break the monopoly of the privately owned Halifax Banking Company). The original staff consisted of cashier (COO) James Forman, tellers Alexander Paul and Benjamin Carlile, and messenger James Maxwell. William Lawson was the bank's first president, serving till 1837.

March 31st

The Habitation at Port Royal.

1713
The Treaty of Utrecht ended the War of Spanish Succession, returning mainland Nova Scotia to the British. Île Royale (Cape Breton) was returned to the French. The British renamed Port Royal as Annapolis Royal. The French would later begin building fortifications at Louisbourg.

1853
The Nova Scotia Railway Company was incorporated. The railway ". . . received a charter to build railway lines from Halifax to Pictou by way of Truro, as well as from Halifax to Victoria Beach, Nova Scotia, on the Annapolis Basin opposite Digby by way of Windsor. The company also received a charter to build from Truro to the border with New Brunswick. The railway was a key project of the visionary Nova Scotian leader Joseph Howe, who felt a government built railway led by Nova Scotia was necessary after the failure of the Intercolonial Railway talks and several fruitless private proposals."

1905
The Royal Navy transferred headquarters of the North American and West Indies Station to Bermuda in preparation for the transfer of the Halifax base to Canada.

APRIL

April 1st

The Wreck of the RMS Atlantic, Currier & Ives, 1873.

1873
The steamer RMS *Atlantic* wrecked off Prospect. It was one of the most disastrous shipwrecks that ever occurred on the North American coast — 546 persons of the 957 onboard died.

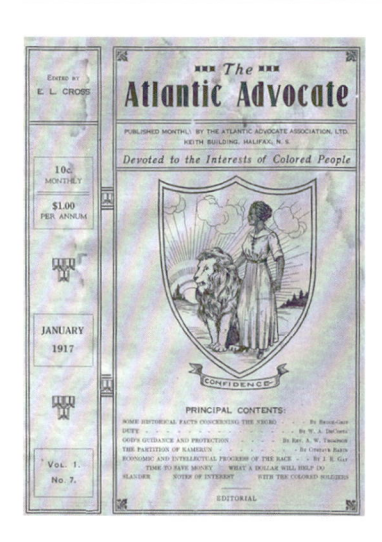

1915
The first issue of the *Atlantic Advocate* appeared. Its masthead read, "Devoted to the interests of colored people." It was published by Wilfred and Miriam DeCosta, and Dr. Clement Courtenay Ligoure. The last issue was published in May 1917.

The Atlantic Advocate (1915–1917).

1996
The Halifax Regional Municipality came into being, amalgamating four municipalities — Halifax, Dartmouth, Bedford and the County of Halifax.

1979
Atlantic Insight Magazine was launched in Halifax by publisher William 'Bill' Belliveau, and editor Harry Bruce.

April 2nd

An official motorcade inaugurated the Angus L. Macdonald Bridge in 1955.

1955
The Angus L. Macdonald Bridge opened. An informative YouTube video on the bridge's construction and subsequent changes can be viewed at: youtube.com/watch?v=358TuJ09S7U (Halifax Dartmouth Bridge Commission, April 6, 2013). The lives of six men were lost during the bridge's initial construction.

1914
Several outside workers at the Drummond Mine had come into the warm boiler room to eat their lunches. They were sitting directly above No. 5 boiler when it blew up, killing seven men.

April 3rd

1823
Lawrence Kavanagh (Kavanah) (1764–1830), took his seat in Legislature. From St. Peter's, Cape Breton, he was a prominent merchant, known as "The Emancipator." He was one of two representatives from Cape Breton, which had joined the mainland House of Assembly in October 1820. He was identified "with the Acadian and Irish." He came from one of the first English-speaking families that settled on Cape Breton Island after the fall of Louisbourg in 1758. He was also the first Roman Catholic to hold a seat in a legislature in the Atlantic Provinces — and did not have to subscribe an oath against popery. He served in the House of Assembly till his death in 1830.

April 4th

The Nova Scotia official flower — the mayflower. (Painting by Maria Morris.)

1987
Chögyam Trungpa Rinpoche died of a cardiac arrest (b. 1939). He had established the Gampo Abbey monastery in Cape Breton in 1983, and his headquarters in Halifax in 1986. He was a supreme abbot of the Surmang monasteries, a scholar, teacher, poet, artist and originator of a radical representation of the Shambhala vision. On the Shambhala tradition, he wrote, "With the great problems facing human society, it seems increasingly important to find simple and non-sectarian ways to work with ourselves and to share our understanding with others. The Shambhala teachings or 'Shambhala vision' as this approach is more broadly called, is one such attempt to encourage a wholesome existence for ourselves and others."

1901
The Floral Emblem Act was assented to, making the mayflower the provincial flower. Early American settlers called it mayflower when they found it growing along the East Coast, because they saw it as the first flower of spring.

1876
The University of Halifax was chartered by the *University Act*, stating that Dalhousie, King's, Mount Saint Vincent and Saint Mary's would be regarded as colleges of the non-sectarian University of Halifax, conferring their degrees in the name University of Halifax. It was meant to be an umbrella institution, like the University of London, England, wherein it would not offer instruction but would examine those who presented themselves and confer degrees if they were successful. But institutional sectarian claims continued to be the preference over collaboration for many years to come.

1866
Queen Victoria wrote in her personal journal: "There will be a great deal to do with the Confederation of N. America which is likely now to be accomplished & which will be a great safeguard against America."

An 1883 painting of Queen Victoria (1819–1901).

April 5th

1874

Charles Macdonald was born and raised in Steam Mill (near Centreville, NS). After his years at sea and some time at home in the Annapolis Valley, his travels took him to the mountains of British Columbia, where he worked on the railroad, explored the terrain and painted a number of watercolours. It was during a period in Vancouver that he joined the Socialist Party of Canada. His interest in architecture was honed during his travels abroad at the turn of the twentieth century when he visited galleries, studied monuments and took in noteworthy structures built of stone and concrete in some major cities of the world. He returned to Nova Scotia in 1910, where he started a concrete brick factory (still not a well-known product), building himself a concrete home (later declared a Provincially Registered Heritage Property). He married Mabel Meisner from Chipman Brook. Between 1934 and 1938, they built five concrete cottages in Huntington Point overlooking the Bay of Fundy, just west of Hall's Harbour, NS. A reporter wrote that the cottages were the sort of structures "in which Snow White and her seven dwarfs might have lived." Macdonald retired in 1951, giving the company to his employees. He died on May 28, 1967. Their residence was turned into the Concrete House Museum and was later run by the Charles Macdonald House of Centreville Society as a Nova Scotia cultural and artistic landmark.

(TOP) The Blue Cottage at Huntington Point, NS, built by Charles Macdonald.
(BOTTOM) The Concrete House Museum, former residence of Charles and Mabel Macdonald, run by the Charles Macdonald House of Centreville Society.

April 5th (cont'd)

The Capture of Louisbourg, 1745, artist unknown.

1745

New England colonial forces, under the command of William Pepperrell (1696–1759) and Commodore Peter Warren (1703–1752), arrived at Canso en route to Louisbourg. They began their attack on May 11. Louisbourg surrendered six weeks later on June 28. One hundred and one New Englanders were killed and over 1,200 would later die of disease and the cold through the winter occupation of 1745–46. The English governor put in charge of the Fort after its surrender, Charles Knowles, wrote, "I have struggled hard to weather the winter, which I've done thank God, tho was not above three times out of my room for five months — I am convinced I shou'd not live out another winter at Louisbourg."

A Plan of the CITY & FORTIFICATIONS OF LOUISBOURG, from a Survey made by Richard Gridley, Lieut. Col. of the Train of Artillery in 1745. (Fortress of Louisbourg.)

April 6th

1779
Henry Alline was ordained in Falmouth. He became a noted evangelist, hymnist and theologian (1748–1784). He arrived with his family from Rhode Island in 1760 to settle in Falmouth, where he became an itinerant preacher and evangelist in rural and frontier Nova Scotia, beginning in 1776. He became a leader in the province of the Great Awakening and the establishment of New Light churches.

1764
The north suburbs of Halifax petitioned to be called Gottingen by application of residents.

April 7th

2014
Mi'kmaw Elder Noel Knockwood died at age eighty-one (b. 1932). Born in Shubenacadie, he was a Korean War veteran and a respected spiritual leader of the Mi'kmaq people. He also served as the first Aboriginal sergeant-at-arms for the Nova Scotia House of Assembly from 2000 to 2005, and served on the Mi'kmaq Grand Council (from 1975). In 2002 he was awarded the National Aboriginal Achievement Award for his efforts to strengthen Mi'kmaq heritage and spirituality.

Noel Knockwood.

April 8th

1820
Sir John Wentworth (1737–1820) died in Halifax at the age of eighty-four. He served as lieutenant governor of Nova Scotia from 1792 to 1808. He had been close friends with John Adams and was also a former governor of New Hampshire. He married Francis Atkinson (1745–1813), née Deering, in 1769 and they were forced to flee Portsmouth, NH, for Halifax in April of 1776 during the American Revolution. However, his wife Francis was not happy with Halifax and had an affair with the visiting Prince William, twenty years her junior. John informed William's father, King George III, of his displeasure, and William was sent back to England. Wentworth would lay the cornerstone for the construction of Government House in 1800.

1943
Paul MacEwan was born in Charlottetown, PEI (d. 2017). He became an MLA for Cape Breton Nova (1970–2003) and later was the Speaker of the Nova Scotia House of Assembly (1993–1996) and an author. He was first elected as an NDP member under the leadership of Jeremy Akerman in 1970. They were the first two NDP MLAs elected in the history of Nova Scotia. MacEwan was expelled from the NDP in 1980 for criticizing a party executive member. He established the Cape Breton Labour Party and was re-elected in 1984. The party ceased operations due to insufficient revenues and MacEwan ran as an independent in 1988 and won. He was admitted to the Liberal party in 1990. He retired in 2003 after having won nine elections in a row — serving thirty-three years in the Nova Scotia Legislature, the longest record of any MLA.

APRIL 9TH

1917

The First World War Battle of Vimy Ridge began on Easter Monday. By April 12, the 85th Battalion (Nova Scotia Highlanders) of the 4th Canadian Division had control of the ridge, capturing Hill 145 in their first battle. The battle had cost the four Canadian divisions 10,602 casualties (3,598 killed and 7,004 wounded). Four members of the Canadian Corps received Victoria Crosses for their actions during the battle. On April 9, 2017, the hundredth anniversary of the Battle of Vimy Ridge was remembered at the Canadian National Vimy Memorial, located on the highest point of the ridge. The Memorial was designed by monument sculptor Walter Allward, constructed over eleven years and unveiled by King Edward VIII on July 26, 1936. It became the centrepiece of a 100-hectare (250-acre) preserved battlefield park — Canada's largest and principal overseas war memorial, dedicated to all Canadians who lost their lives in the First World War. The names of 11,285 Canadian soldiers who have no known grave in France were also etched on the forward wall of the monument.

Four months after the Battle of Vimy Ridge, from August 15 to 25, another major battle pitted the Canadian Corps against five divisions of the German 6th Army at Hill 70 (or Sallaumines Hill, near the industrial coal city of Lens, France). The Canadians took the hill and held it. 8,677 Canadian soldiers were killed, wounded or missing in the ten-day battle. German losses were between 12,000 and 20,000. Six Victoria Crosses were awarded to Canadian soldiers.

(TOP) The Battle of Vimy Ridge, *by Richard Jack, 1918.*
(BOTTOM) Ghosts of Vimy Ridge *by William Longstaff.*

April 10th

(LEFT) St. George's (Anglican) Round Church as seen from the tower of St. Patrick's (Roman Catholic) Church, 1957.
(RIGHT) Modern-day view of St. George's.

1800

The cornerstone of St. George's (Anglican) Round Church was laid by Sir John Wentworth — a cylindrical wooden church designed in the Georgian style with Palladian elements. The design was a concept from Edward, the Duke of Kent, who was commander of the British forces in Nova Scotia at the time. He was a son of King George III, and played an active role in the planning of the new building. Though the first service would be held in July 1801, the building was not completed until 1812. It is recognized as the first round church built in North America and the only Georgian round church built of wood. An early parishioner, J.F.W. DesBarres, the famous Nova Scotian cartographer and former governor of Cape Breton, was buried with his wife Martha in a double crypt beneath St. George's. This was the only crypt beneath St. George's. In June 1994, a fire destroyed 40 per cent of the structure. But with support from across the country and the world, St. George's rose again!

1841

The City of Halifax was incorporated. The original Mi'kmaq name for the area was K'jipuktuk. Earlier versions used Chebookt, meaning chief bay or harbour. The area was considered sacred by the Mi'kmaq, who used it for camping and trading. In 1749, 2,547 settlers from England, Ireland and Scotland arrived (also see; Cornwallis, June 21, 1749). A third of the settlers who arrived didn't make it through the first winter, and many left for New England. Later, others arrived from New England, as well as German "Foreign Protestants," planters and African-American slaves, followed by Loyalists, free Black Loyalists and Irish Catholics. Prior to 1841, civic administration was managed by governors and magistrates appointed by Britain, with justices of the peace managing local affairs and legal duties. The first officials of the City of Halifax were elected on May 12, 1841. By Confederation (1867), Halifax was the fourth-largest city in Canada. On April 1, 1996, city governance underwent a significant change when the City of Halifax amalgamated with the City of Dartmouth, the Municipality of the County of Halifax and the Town of Bedford to form the Halifax Regional Municipality (HRM), totalling a population of 403,131 (2017).

APRIL 10TH (CONT'D)

1989
The Maritime Music Awards (later called the East Coast Music Awards — ECMAs, in 1991) were first staged at the Flamingo Café and Lounge in Halifax. There were nine award categories. Musician John Gracie was the inaugural winner for Male Artist of the Year in 1989.

John Gracie.

1930
Legislation that created the Nova Scotia Police came into force. The force was eventually organized into seven districts and comprised almost one hundred officers. But by April 1, 1932, due to increased costs, the NS government entered into an agreement with the RCMP to take over provincial policing, with most members of the Nova Scotia Police being absorbed by the federal force. The RCMP assigned 175 officers to Nova Scotia. As of 2017, the RCMP "H" Division had 1,500 employees in thirty-eight detachments throughout Nova Scotia.

APRIL 11TH

1885
The Halifax Provisional Battalion left Halifax to fight in the North-West Rebellion against a force of Métis under Gabriel Dumont. Under the command of Lieutenant-Colonel James J. Bremner, the battalion would be gone for three months. The wrought-iron gates at the Halifax Public Gardens were made in the battalion's honour.

The Halifax Provisional Battalion in Medicine Hat, District of Assiniboia (1885).

2016
Bay Ferries Ltd. released its fees for their high-speed Nova Scotia-to-Maine ferry service. Nova Scotia taxpayers were expected to support the service for $32.7 million over two years to refloat the previous ferry service, including a ten-year agreement to cover any cash deficiencies the company might incur — if Bay Ferries lost money, those losses were to be reimbursed by taxpayers. A previous operator, Nova Star Cruises, failed to meet passenger targets and used up $39.5 million in provincial subsidies during its two-year service (as reported by the CBC). Bay Ferries began service on June 15.

April 11th (cont'd)

2016
Mi'kmaw educator Elsie J. Basque died (b. in the Acadian community of Clare, Digby County, May 12, 1916). She was a graduate of the Provincial Normal College in Truro (1937), the first Mi'kmaw person to receive a teacher's licence and to teach in a non-native school. She was a recipient of the Order of Canada in 2013.

1914
Birth of Robert L. Stanfield (d. 2003). He was the seventeenth premier of Nova Scotia (1956–1967) and later the leader of the federal Progressive Conservative Party of Canada. A graduate of Dalhousie University and Harvard Law School in the 1930s, Stanfield became the leader of the Nova Scotia Progressive Conservative Party in 1948 and, after a rebuilding period, led the party to government in 1956, going on to win three straight elections.

April 12th

1791
Provo William Parry Wallis was born in Halifax (d. 1892). He became a notable Royal Navy officer who took part in the capture of the USS *Chesapeake* by the frigate HMS *Shannon*. After many exploits at sea and in battle, he became Admiral of the British Fleet in 1875 and died at the age of one hundred. (Also see The victorious Royal Navy, June 6, 1813.)

Sir Provo William Parry Wallis (1791–1892), painted by Robert Field, c 1813.

1918
Grand Chief John Denny Jr. died. Born on the Eskasoni reserve in 1841, he served the Mi'kmaq people for thirty-seven years. He was the last of the Mi'kmaq hereditary grand chiefs — he was the son of Grand Chief John Denny and Elizabeth Marshall, and the great-grandson of Grand Chief Toma Dennis.

1861
The American Civil War began (1861–1865). It would claim over 750,000 Union and Confederate soldiers and an undetermined number of civilians. Over two hundred Nova Scotians who fought in the war (est. 40,000 Canadians) have been identified, but it is thought that up to two thousand men migrated to the US before 1860.

April 12th (cont'd)

J. Allister Bowman, district plant superintendent, Maritime Tel & Tel, using earphones to listen for entombed men.

1936

The Moose River Gold Mine disaster occurred. "The roof of the mine collapsed, trapping three men, Herman Magill, Dr. David Robertson and Alfred Scadding, 150 feet down for 11 days. The men were reached by drilling a borehole on the sixth day to send food, water and a telephone till the rescue was completed. Robertson and Scadding survived and Magill died on the seventh day. The event was broadcast by J. Frank Willis of the Canadian Radio Broadcasting Commission (CRBC) to over 650 radio stations throughout North America, with an estimated 100 million listeners. It was also picked up by the BBC and broadcast to Europe. It was the first live 24-hour radio coverage of a breaking news story in Canada."(Creative Commons.)

Promotional material for the Hollywood B-movie based on the disaster, called Draegerman Courage.

April 13th

1905

Robert William Chambers was born in Wolfville. He loved drawing as a child. He later became a well-loved, award-winning editorial cartoonist whose work spanned a fifty-three-year career, appearing regularly in the *Chronicle Herald*. In the early 1920s, he studied art in New York, returning to Nova Scotia in 1932 to work as an editorial cartoonist. He died in 1996, two weeks before his ninety-first birthday. A range of his work can be viewed online at bobchamberscartoons.blogspot.ca.

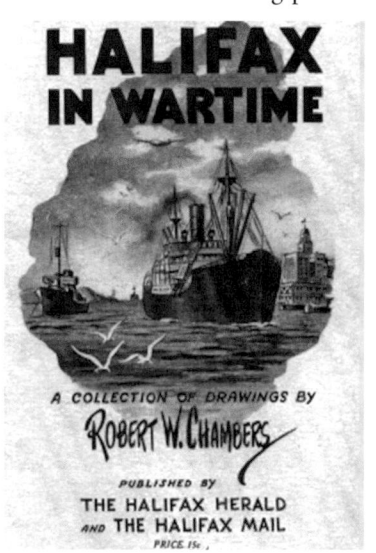

(TOP LEFT) Bob Chambers, 1941. (RIGHT) A collection of Bob's drawings.

1954

Premier Angus L. Macdonald died while in office (b. 1890). A First World War veteran, "He served as the Liberal premier of Nova Scotia from 1933 to 1940, when he became the federal minister of defence for naval services. He oversaw the creation of an effective Canadian navy and Allied convoy service during World War II." After the Second World War, he returned to Nova Scotia from Ottawa and was elected premier once again in 1945.

Angus L. Macdonald (centre) with his brothers, Oswin (left) and John Colin (right). Macdonald was seriously wounded by a German sniper only four days before the armistice.

April 14th

1912

The largest passenger steamship in the world, *Titanic*, collided with an iceberg at 11:40 p.m. during her maiden voyage from Southampton to New York City. Of 2,224 passengers and crew aboard, more than 1,500 died in the sinking (including 132 Canadians), making it one of the deadliest commercial peacetime maritime disasters in modern history. One hundred and fifty *Titanic* victims were buried in Halifax in the Fairview Lawn, Mount Olivet and Baron de Hirch/Beth Israel Synagogue cemeteries — which the Nova Scotia Museum states is the largest number anywhere in the world.

A composite image of the Titanic *(foreground) with a contemporary cruise ship.*

April 15th

1924

Murdock Maxwell MacOrdum (1901–1955) submitted his MA thesis, entitled *Survivals of English and Scottish Popular Ballads in Nova Scotia: A Study of Folk Song in Canada*, at McGill University. He was inspired and influenced by William Roy Mackenzie's book *The Quest of the Ballad*. (Also see William Roy Mackenzie, February. 14, 1883.) Dr. Helen Creighton would likewise be influenced by both Mackenzie's and MacOrdum's work. MacOrdum was born in Marion Bridge. He would become president of Carleton College (1947–1955). The library at Carleton University was named after him.

1923

"Keep to the Right" was instituted on NS highways, thereby changing from left-hand drive.

April 16th

2013

Rita MacNeil died (b. in Big Pond, Cape Breton, in 1944). Starting in 1975, she released twenty-six albums and won dozens of awards over her musical career. She was also a Member of the Order of Canada (1992) and the Order of Nova Scotia (2005).

Rita MacNeil.

1930

Jerry Lonecloud died. Also known as Germain (or Jeremiah) Bartlett Alexis, Jerry Bartlett or in Mi'kmaq as Slme'n Laksi (Haselmah Luxcey), he was born in Belfast, Maine, in 1854 and became a well-known Mi'kmaw guide, herbalist and folklorist. Both his parents were from Nova Scotia and he later settled for a time in Bear River. He passed on many oral histories and folk tales to Harry Piers, curator of the Provincial Museum (see January 24, 1940), and to Clarissa Archibald Dennis (see February 26, 1958). His grandfather (Tom Philips) had been a native hunting guide for British army officers garrisoned at Halifax. He travelled in Buffalo Bill's Wild West Show and Healey and Bigelow's Medicine Show — where he was give the name "Dr. Lone Cloud." He had lived in Liscomb, and then later in the Tufts Cove/Turtle Grove area where he lost two daughters in the Halifax Explosion. He also lost one eye and all his possessions. Historian Ruth Holmes Whitehead wrote of Lonecloud, "Ethnographer of the Micmac nation could rightly have been his epitaph, his final honour."

Jerry Lonecloud (1854–1930), well-known Mi'kmaw guide, herbalist and folklorist.

1945

The minesweeper HMCS *Esquimalt* was sunk by *U-190*, a German U-boat, a few miles off Chebucto Head. It sank in five minutes with the loss of thirty-nine men. It was the last Canadian warship to suffer that fate during the Second World War.

HMCS Esquimalt.

April 17th

2011
Award-winning artist Joseph Purcell (b. 1927) was honoured in a ceremony organized by the Saint Patrick's Church Restoration Society, held at Saint Patrick's Church in Halifax. In 1951, Purcell painted a series of murals high above the high altar at the church. Joseph and his wife, Tela, were married in the church, as were his parents and grandparents. From age fifteen, Purcell developed an early interest in painting and exhibiting his work.

Oldham, *by Joseph Purcell.*

1915
First World War prisoners began to arrive at the Amherst Prisoner-of-War (POW) Internment Camp from Halifax aboard armed trains. The camp was the largest POW camp in Canada during the war — holding a maximum of 854 prisoners. Besides Amherst, there were also internment camps at Melville Island on the Northwest Arm of Halifax, and at Citadel Hill (Fort George). There were twenty-four camps across the country. The Amherst camp closed on September 27, 1919. One notable prisoner at the camp was Russian leader Leon Trotsky (1879–1940), who arrived there in early April of 1917. He was released at the end of April and would go back to Russia, where he and Vladimir Lenin (1870–1924) began the 1917 October Revolution. Author and playwright Silver Donald Cameron's play about Trotsky's confinement as a POW in Amherst is called *The Prophet at Tantramar* (1988).

Russian leader Leon Trotsky.

1969
The *4th ESTATE* newspaper began publishing. It was created when father and son team Frank and Nick Fillmore left a still less-than-a-year-old paper called *The People* to form their own paper. At the time, it was considered a "radical" newspaper, providing a feisty and combative tone to many stories that impacted people across Nova Scotia. It published till 1977.

The 4th ESTATE *newspaper.*

April 18th

1958

The Nova Scotia Government and General Employees Union (NSGEU) opened its founding convention, with ninety-five delegates representing thirteen divisions with occupational and regional representation. The NSGEU is an active affiliate of the Nova Scotia Federation of Labour, the National Union of Public and General Employees and the Canadian Labour Congress. It represents over 31,000 public and private sector employees in Nova Scotia.

April 19th

1864

Nova Scotia became the first province to pass legislation, the *Free Schools Act,* to remove schools from "dependency on charity by guaranteeing a free education" for all Nova Scotia children. By 1883, "local school boards were permitted to oblige children between seven and 12 to attend school for at least 80 days per year and to fine parents who did not send their children to school."

April 20th

(TOP) George Henry Wright (1849–1912).
(LEFT) Local Council of Women House, Young Avenue, gift of George Wright, as it looked in 1999.

1912

The *Chronicle Herald* confirmed that well-known Halifax property developer and philanthropist George Henry Wright (b. 1849) had died on the ill-fated voyage of the *Titanic*, age sixty-three. His body was not recovered. His will left his residence on the corner of Inglis and Young Street (number 689) to the Council of Women of Halifax to further the cause of women's suffrage (their right to vote), and the rest to relatives.

April 20th (cont'd)

2014
Author Alistair MacLeod died (b. North Battleford, SK, July 20, 1936). He was an award-winning author and academic whose stories evoked the beauty of Cape Breton and its resilient characters. His book *No Great Mischief* (1999) was voted Atlantic Canada's greatest book of all time. It also won the 2001 IMPAC Dublin Literary Award. "I think we should realize that 'story' is much older than literacy, you know, and that all kinds of people tell stories who can't read and write. But I think that as a writer . . . I like to give the impression that I am telling the story rather than writing the story."
– Alistair MacLeod (from: Robert Jarovi. "An Interview with Alistair MacLeod," *The Scots Canadian,* Vol. 5, February 2002)

1970
While searching for the crew of the missing herring seiner *Enterprise*, the CN rail ferry *Patrick Morris* sank off Cape Breton during a vicious gale. Forty-seven crew were rescued, but the captain, Roland Perry, aged fifty-four, and three officers were lost. The *Enterprise* crew of eight were also lost.

April 21st

1947
Agnes Dennis died (b. 1859). A former president of the Victorian Order of Nurses (VON), from 1901 to 1946, and the Red Cross, she mobilized nurses and relief efforts during the First World War. She also helped in coordinating assistance after the Halifax Explosion in 1917. She was considered part of a growing cadre of affluent, educated and experienced Nova Scotian women who sought social change for women. She was the mother of ten children. One of her daughters was Clarissa (Clara) Archibald Dennis, a noted photographer and journalist in the '30s. (Also see Clarissa Dennis, February. 26, 1958.) Her husband, William, began work as a reporter with the *Halifax Herald* (1875–1881) and became editor-in-chief and president in 1890.

Agnes Dennis and her husband, William.

April 22nd

1910
Maritime Telegraph & Telephone Company was incorporated. By 1998, it merged with the Island Telephone Company (PEI), NBTel and NewTel Communications (NL) to form Aliant — or Bell Aliant.

APRIL 23RD

David Woods.

2016
Nova Scotian award-winning visual artist, curator, poet, playwright, arts founder/organizer, director and writer David Woods received the 2016 Harry Jerome Award for Entertainment by the Black Business and Professional Association of Canada. Born in Trinidad in 1959, Woods immigrated with his parents and four siblings to Dartmouth in 1972. "As a teenager, Woods was a gifted student and initially planned a career in law, but after working with Black youth in Preston he turned his attention to creating drama and performance, literature and painting as a way of capturing the stories of Nova Scotia's Black communities which he felt were being ignored by history." (*Pride News*.)

1762
Joshua Mauger (1725–1788) was appointed Nova Scotia Agent in London. By December 1763 he was no longer the agent, though "he remained the colony's unofficial spokesman, with more apparent influence than a succession of governors." Besides being active in the Halifax liquor trade, Mauger was also involved in the slave trade.

Just imported and to be sold by Joshua Mauger.

1851
Canada's first official stamp, the Three-Pence Beaver, was issued — designed by Sandford Fleming (age twenty-four). (Also see Sandford Fleming, July 22, 1915.)

Canada's first stamp — The Three-Pence Beaver, designed by Sir Sandford Fleming.

1826
Construction began on the Shubenacadie Canal and waterway with the arrival of forty-four Irish stonemasons from Scotland, all experienced in the construction of British-style granite locks. Labourers — many of them also essentially stonemasons — were also brought in from Ireland. The remnants of their work camps were left along the canal as it winds its way through Dartmouth's Shubie Park.

APRIL 24TH

1895
Mount Hanley, Annapolis County, native Joshua Slocum (b. 1844) set out from Boston in the *Spray* on his voyage around the world. He would arrive back at Newport, Rhode Island, on June 27, 1898, after a voyage of 46,000 miles. He published a best-selling memoir on his journey in 1900 — *Sailing Alone Around the World*.

Joshua Slocum. He protected himself from pirates by spreading carpet tacks on his deck every night before going to sleep.

APRIL 25TH

1894
Annie Isabella Hamilton (1866–1941) became the first woman to graduate from Dalhousie Medical School. She worked closely with Dr. Maria Louisa Angwin (1849–1898), a Newfoundland-born, US-trained doctor, who became the first woman licenced to practice medicine in Nova Scotia, and a dedicated feminist. Annie practised medicine in the North End of Halifax for about a decade before deciding to emigrate to China as a medical missionary in 1903 (she had learned Chinese while studying at Dalhousie and had been a member of the Knox Presbyterian Church in Brookfield). She lived in China till her death in Shanghai in 1941.

Annie Isabella Hamilton.

1978
The Maritime Sikh Society was incorporated in Nova Scotia and aided in the building of the Sikh Gurdwara (a place of worship), opened in Halifax on November 19, 1978 — the only Gurdwara east of Montreal (the foundation stone was laid June 4, 1978).

APRIL 26TH

1918
The *Nova Scotia Franchise Act* received royal assent in Nova Scotia — women were granted the right to vote in provincial elections, the first province to do so in Atlantic Canada (this did not include Indigenous women). A month later, the federal government, under Prime Minister Robert Borden, passed legislation for the whole country to allow women to vote. It wouldn't be till 1953 that Nova Scotia enacted fair employment laws, and 1956 that the province enacted equal pay legislation. The *Human Rights Act* was enacted in 1962. (Also see Eliza Ritchie, September 5, 1933.)

April 27th

2017
Bill No. 59, *An Act Respecting Accessibility in Nova Scotia* completed Third Reading and became law. First introduced on November 2, 2016, by Minister of Community Services Joanne Bernard, the bill went through a series of public consultations, meetings and amendments. With the *Act* passed, the Nova Scotia Department of Justice was deemed responsible for accessibility compliance and enforcement.

April 28th

1827
William Hall was born (d. 1904.) (Also see William Hall, November 16, 1857.) He was the son of Jacob and Lucy Hall, former slaves who fled the US and landed in Halifax as refugees of the War of 1812. The Halls eventually moved to Horton Bluff, on the Minas Basin in Nova Scotia, where William and six other children were born. Hall joined the British Navy in 1852, obtaining the Victoria Cross in 1857, and served till 1876. When he retired, he moved to a small farmhouse near Hantsport.

April 29th

1863
Dalhousie College was re-established. Though founded in 1818 by Lord Dalhousie, when he was later appointed governor general of Canada his influence waned, and the college did not actually offer a consistent program of studies till 1838. The program was only offered intermittently till 1863 when the college was reorganized and opened with six professors to undertake teaching efforts. The first degrees were offered in 1866, with twenty-eight students for degrees and twenty-eight occasional students.

April 30th

1900
David Joseph Manners (born Rauff de Ryther Duan Acklom) was born in Halifax. He moved with his family to New York City as a young boy and later became a well-known actor in Hollywood during the beginning of the talking film era. One of his most notable roles was that of Jonathan Harker in the 1931 film *Dracula*, which also starred Bela Lugosi in the title role. He retired from screen acting in 1936, performing occasionally on stage, and writing. He died in 1998 at the age of ninety-eight in Santa Barbara, California.

David Manners performing with the young Katharine Hepburn in A Bill of Divorcement *(1932).*

MAY

MAY 1ST

The Conservatory, by Francis M. Jones Bannerman (1883).

1883
Nova Scotia artist Frances Jones Bannerman (1855–1944), was the first Canadian artist to exhibit her work at the Paris Salon. She was one of the first North American artists to incorporate impressionism into her paintings. She was the daughter of the Honourable Alfred Alpin Jones (1824–1906), a successful Halifax-based businessman, who served as lieutenant governor of Nova Scotia from 1900 to 1906. In 1886, Frances married a fellow artist, Englishman Hamlet Bannerman.

1896
Sir Charles Tupper (1821–1915) formed the federal government in Ottawa as the sixth prime minister of Canada seven days after Parliament had been dissolved. He had led Nova Scotia into Confederation and was Premier of Nova Scotia from 1864 to 1867. He lost the June 23 election and resigned on July 8, 1896, making his sixty-nine day term as prime minister the shortest in Canadian history. He became the last living Father of Confederation.

May 2nd

1927
Award-winning Nova Scotian author Budge Wilson was born in Halifax. Author of thirty-four books, she started being published in 1984, with many of her works encompassing stories for young people. She won over twenty-three Canadian Children's Book Centre "Our Choice" selections, as well as a Canadian Library Association Young Adult Book Award and many other recognitions. She was appointed a Member of the Order of Canada in 2004, and the Order of Nova Scotia in 2011.

1797
Abraham Gesner (d. 1864) was born at Chipman Corner. He was a noted geologist, inventor, physician, surgeon and the discoverer of kerosene. He received patents on kerosene from US Patent Office on June 27, 1854.

May 3rd

1933
Judson Graham Day was born in Halifax. After appearing as a singer on *Singalong Jubilee*, he went on to become a corporate lawyer and a director of numerous companies, serving as chairman and CEO of British Shipbuilders in the mid-80s and later the Rover Group, and in Canada, was a chairman of Hydro-One. He was knighted by Queen Elizabeth II in 1989, received the Order of Nova Scotia in 2011, and appointed an Officer of the Order of Canada in 2014.

Graham Day (centre) received the Order of Nova Scotia (2011).

2017
Father Greg MacLeod died in Sydney (b. in Sydney Mines, 1935). He was a lifelong educator, ordained a Roman Catholic priest in 1961 and become involved in community economic development initiatives in Cape Breton. He founded the Tompkins Institute in 1974 at the University College of Cape Breton (now Cape Breton University — CBU) and had a close association with the founding of CBU's Centre for Community Economic Development in 1986.

He is best known as the founder of New Dawn Enterprises in 1976, the oldest community development corporation in Canada, involved in business and social development in Cape Breton. He was the leading visionary behind BCA Investment Cooperative Ltd. (part of the BCA Group), established in 1998. He authored many articles, as well as the book *From Mondragon to America: Experiments in Community Economic Development* (Cape Breton University Press, 1997).

Father Greg Macleod.

May 4th

1783
The first fleet of four hundred settlers from New York arrived at Port Roseway, among them, disbanded soldiers and black regiments. Soon the area's population would swell to between 9,000 and 10,000 refugees.

1913
A fire in North Sydney destroyed over forty-one businesses. It was noted to be similar to a fire that took place in December of 1881.

May 5th

1783
J.F.W. DesBarres' *Atlantic Neptune* charts of Nova Scotia were advertised for sale by Thomas Freeman, Halifax. Considered ". . . the most important collection of maps, charts and views of North America published in the eighteenth century." Four editions of the folios were published — 1777, 1780, 1781 and 1784 — that covered different geographic areas from the coasts of Nova Scotia to New England, to the coasts and harbours of the St. Lawrence and, lastly, New York, south and west to the Gulf of Mexico.

1892
Edwin Borden (1869–1953) was the first African Nova Scotian to graduate from Acadia University. He was also among the first athletes of African descent to graduate from a Canadian university. He went on to complete his master's and doctorate degrees.

May 6th

1985
Academy Award–winning actress (and six-time nominee) Shirley MacLaine received an honorary doctorate from Acadia University. MacLaine's mother, Kathlyn Corinne (née MacLean) was a drama teacher who had been born in Wolfville and educated at Acadia (1928). Her grandmother was also a former dean of women at Acadia. MacLaine grew up in Wolfville till the age of twelve when she moved with her family to the United States. Sister to well-known actor Warren Beatty.

Former Wolfville resident and Academy Award–winning actress Shirley MacLaine, c. 1987.

May 6th (cont'd)

1815
Black refugees (upwards of 200) from the War of 1812 Chesapeake Bay area were quarantined on Melville Island due to concerns about the spread of disease. Many later settled in Hammonds Plains, Beechville, Lucasville and the Campbell Road Settlement area, which later became known as Africville (est. in 1848). Gabriel Hall was amongst those who arrived at that time.

(LEFT) Melville Island Prison, c.1900. (RIGHT) Gabriel Hall, in the only known image of a black refugee from the War of 1812.

2014
Sinclair Williams of East Preston died (age seventy-one). He was the first black police officer in Dartmouth. At age twenty-five he was hired in July of 1968. Looking back over the years, a fellow officer, George Beck, said of Williams, "He would take the lead as a senior officer so I learned so much in the way he would handle the calls at the initial state and, generally, becoming a good policeman." The Williams family established a memorial scholarship in his name to benefit black students going into policing.

May 7th

1980
Terry Fox arrived in North Sydney from Port aux Basques on his cross-country Marathon of Hope. Due to his illness, he had to stop the marathon on September 1 in Thunder Bay.

Terry Fox.

MAY 7TH (CONT'D)

The unofficial VE Day celebrations and riots in Halifax, May 7–8, 1945.

1945
Germany surrendered and VE Day Riots occurred on May 7 to 8 in Halifax. Several thousand servicemen, merchant seamen and civilians went on a looting rampage of the City of Halifax. Twenty-five thousand servicemen were in the city at the time and wanted to celebrate the war's end — the only problem was authorities decided to shut down the liquor commission outlets to prevent "trouble," and restaurants, retailers, and movie theatres followed suit.

2011
Harry Bruce was awarded the Lifetime Achievement Award at the 2011 Atlantic Journalism Awards. His family roots in Nova Scotia stretch back to the late eighteenth century. He began his journalism career in 1955 in Ottawa, later working for *Maclean's, Saturday Night,* the *Canadian,* and the *Star Weekly.* Moving to Nova Scotia in 1971, he wrote for national and regional newspapers and magazines. He was the founding editor of *Atlantic Insight Magazine* in April 1979. He authored over sixteen books, winning numerous awards. Author Silver Donald Cameron wrote of Harry, "He's been a self-sustaining professional journalist for more than half a century, an inspiration to all those who aspire to support themselves by their skill and intelligence."

Harry Bruce.

1915
While en route from New York to Liverpool, England, the Cunard liner RMS *Lusitania* was torpedoed and sunk off the coast of Ireland by a German submarine, U-20, with 1,198 lives lost. Fears for the safety of *Lusitania* and other liners that also sailed from ports such as Halifax ran high during this time due to the state of war with Germany. There were a number of Canadians as well as American citizens, onboard the ship. It was argued that the sinking shifted public opinion which led The United States to join the war two years later.

MAY 8TH

1756
Mi'kmaq and Maliseet warriors raided two islands on the northern outskirts of the fortified Township of Lunenburg, (John) Rous Island and Payzant Island (later renamed Covey Island). French reports tell of twenty settlers being killed and five taken prisoner. This raid was the first of nine the warriors would conduct against the peninsula over a three-year period. Louis Payzant was killed in one attack, while his wife, Marie-Anne, and their four children were kidnapped to Aukpaque (near what became Fredericton, NB), and taken later to Quebec. They returned to Nova Scotia in 1759 and settled in the Falmouth area. His son, John Payzant (1749–1834), would later write of his experiences being held captive. By 1756, the Halifax settlement was enclosed within a line of forts and batteries. (Also See Gov. Charles Lawrence... May14, 1756.)

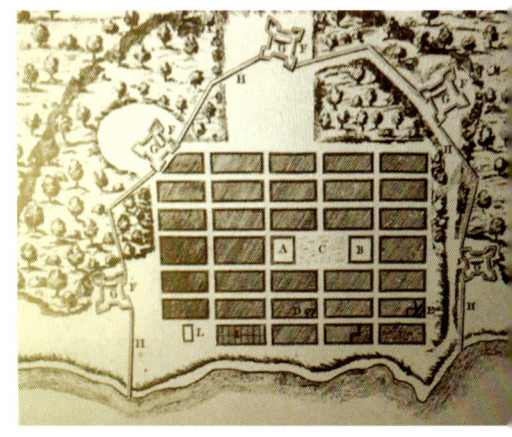

John Brewse's plan for fortifying Halifax, 1749.

2013
Bill Langstroth died (b. 1930). He was a well-known musician, artist, writer, photographer and CBC producer. After a brief stint in the navy, he worked as a producer for CBC-TV in the 1950s in Halifax on *The Don Messer Show,* and later produced and co-hosted *Singalong Jubilee.* He continued to work for CBC in Halifax and later in Toronto for over forty years. In 2011, Langstroth was inducted into the Canadian Country Music Hall of Fame.

1834
The Irish immigrant ship *Astrea* ran aground near the community of Little Lorraine, Cape Breton — 248 lives were lost.

MAY 9TH

1864
Irish-born Canadian artist Forshaw Day (1831–1903) presented his work, *The Waverley Goldfields, Nova Scotia*, at the international Dublin exhibition. Gold had been discovered in Waverley in 1861 and the Waverley Gold Mining Company included Day's work in the provincial submission to the exhibition. Day had arrived in Halifax in 1862, opening a studio in the city and teaching art for a number of years. He later taught drawing at the Royal Military College in Kingston. In 1880 he was a founding member of the Royal Canadian Academy of Arts.

The Waverley Goldfields, Nova Scotia c. 1865, by Forshaw Day.

400 YEARS IN 365 DAYS

May 9th (cont'd)

The Halifax Municipal Airport, 1931.

1931
The first recorded flight at the Halifax Airport, Chebucto Road, took place — now known as Saunders Park in the West End of Halifax.

1758
Admiral Edward Boscawen (1711–1761), with his fleet and troops under the command of General Jeffery Amherst, arrived in Halifax from England prior to the planned British attack on Fortress Louisbourg. Also with him was Brigadier General James Wolfe. The fleet consisted of 120 transport ships, twenty-three ships of the line and eighteen frigates, with a total combined army and naval force of over 27,000. They would spend the month in Halifax preparing plans for their attack on Louisbourg. General Amherst did not arrive till the fleet set sail from Halifax on May 29. They would capture Fortress Louisbourg on July 27.

1992
At 5:18 a.m. the Westray mining disaster occurred in Plymouth, Pictou County, killing the entire shift of twenty-six miners. Many people in the area felt their homes shake as a result of the explosion. It was Canada's worst mining disaster since the Springhill mining disaster in 1958 that claimed seventy-five miners. The Westray mine opened in September 1991 and was owned and managed by Curragh Resources Inc. Of the twenty-six killed, eleven bodies were never recovered. Over a million dollars was raised in donations to the Westray Families Group, which was put aside to help the forty-two children who lost their fathers in the disaster. A list of those who died at Westray was published at: NovaScotia.ca/lae/pubs/westray/execsumm.asp. Alexa McDonough, leader of the Nova Scotia NDP Party at that time, said of the tragedy, "This was no act of God. This was an act of public policy." On May 15, 1992, Justice K. Peter Richard was asked by the provincial government to conduct a public enquiry into the disaster. (Also see Westray, December 1, 1997.)

1914
Hank Snow was born in Brooklyn, Queens County, NS. He grew up in Liverpool. He later became a celebrated Canadian and US country music artist, known as The Yodelling Ranger and The Singing Ranger. He got his start performing live on CHNS radio in Halifax. Later he began touring and went to Nashville. He had a career spanning fifty years, 140 albums and eighty-five singles on *Billboard* from 1950 to 1980. He died in Nashville in 1999.

Hank Snow.

May 10th

1773

The British Parliament passed the *Tea Act*, taxing the US colonies. By December 16, it would ignite the American Revolution when the Sons of Liberty, disguised as Mohawk Indians, boarded three ships in Boston Harbour and destroyed 92,000 pounds of British East India Company tea. Within ten years, in the heat of the American conflict, Nova Scotia would receive a flood of more than 25,000 Loyalist refugees, adding to the population of over 12,000 inhabitants of British origin in the colony.

A view of . . . Boston . . . and Brittish [sic] Ships of War . . . 1768, by Paul Revere.

1758

Building the Halifax Dockyard, or the Royal Naval Dockyard as it was also known, began under the supervision of James Cook. He had arrived with Admiral Boscawen in preparation for the British attack on Louisbourg (see Boscawen, May 9, 1758). It was the first royal dockyard in North America, officially commissioned in 1759. The dockyard was designated a national historic site of Canada in 1923 and part of Canadian Forces Base (CFB) Halifax — the largest military base in Canada, with 7,500 military and 2,300 civilian employees.

May 11th

1936

Edith Jessie Archibald died in Halifax (b. 1854). She was a leading feminist of her time, a writer and novelist who led the Maritime Women's Christian Temperance Union, the National Council of Women of Canada and the Local Council of Women of Halifax. From 1897 to 1901 she was president of the Halifax VON (Victoria Order of Nurses), and served as vice-president of the NS Red Cross in 1914, chairing the department responsible for Canadian prisoners of war overseas. She later chaired the Halifax Conservative Women's Auxillary. Her father was Sir Edward Mortimer, of whom she wrote a biography in 1924. In 1997 she was designated a Person of National Historic Significance by the Government of Canada.

1891

Noted Nova Scotian author, historian and First World War veteran Will R. Bird was born in East Mapleton, Cumberland County. He was the author of twenty-five books and 600 short stories. Many were historical fiction, war stories, memoirs and travel accounts.

MAY 12TH

Actor Austin Willis and pianist Dick Fry performed from the CHNS Studio in the Lord Nelson Hotel, 1928.

1926

Nova Scotia's first radio station, CHNS, broadcast for the first time from a tiny room at the Carleton Hotel in Halifax using a 500-watt transmitter. The station was created by the Halifax Radio Listeners' Club with technical assistance from the Northern Electric Co. Later in November, Bill Borrett, who also was a member of the club, would do the first live hockey broadcast. Later that year, station ownership came under the Halifax-Herald Ltd. By 1928, the station moved to the top of the Lord Nelson Hotel. The NS Department of Education began hosting educational broadcasts on March 19, 1928.

1802

King's College in Windsor received a royal charter from King George III, becoming the first university in what would become Canada. It was founded in November 1788 as the King's Collegiate School by resettled Anglican Loyalists as a boys' residential school (called the Academy). In 1788, it opened with seventeen students. A year later, the University of King's College emerged from the collegiate. A major fire would occur in February of 1920, and it was decided to move the college to Halifax in 1923, leaving the boys' collegiate at the original site in Windsor. In 1976, the school amalgamated with the girls' Edgehill School to form King's-Edgehill School, receiving royal assent in 1982. The University of King's College in Halifax is the oldest chartered university in Canada and the first English-speaking university in the Commonwealth outside the UK. The former site of King's College in Windsor was designated a National Historic Site of Canada on May 25, 1923.

MAY 13TH

1770
With encouragement from Michael Francklin (lieutenant governor of Nova Scotia from 1766 to 1772), the Mi'kmaq restored their celebrations of Saint Aspinquid, in what became Point Pleasant Park in Halifax. It was an annual festival of old times, now lost, that recognized a faithful Mi'kmaq chief named Aspinquid (Aspenquid) who had converted to Catholicism. Saint Aspinquid appeared in the Nova Scotia almanacs from 1774 to 1786. The festival also has its roots in the Mi'kmaq Old Spring Feast, which was celebrated on or immediately after the last quarter of the moon in the month of May, when the tide was low. There was a Saint Aspinquid's Chapel and a burial ground associated with the area. In the 1750s, Michael Francklin had been a prisoner of the Mi'kmaq, and over six months in captivity he learned some of the rudiments of their language and their culture.

1751
Sixty Mi'kmaq warriors and Acadian insurgents attacked the Dartmouth settlement, leaving twenty settlers killed and scalped. Some were also taken prisoner. Bodies were later taken to Halifax and buried in the Old Burying Ground. Governor Cornwallis reported to his superiors on the attack (June 24, 1751), expressing his frustration with the poor protection his soldiers had provided. A wooden palisade was subsequently built around the vulnerable settlement. A ferryman, John Connor, was granted permission to provide a ferry service between the Dartmouth and Halifax settlements in February 1752.

The Cape Breton Causeway.

1955
The Cape Breton Causeway opened with 40,000 people in attendance and twenty-five lines of pipers.

1861
Margaret M. Saunders was born in Berwick (d. 1947). She was an author of children's stories and romance novels, as well as the million-plus bestseller *Beautiful Joe* (1894).

MAY 14TH

1847
Sir Frederick Borden, Canadian Minister of Militia and Defence (1896–1911), was born at Cornwallis. He was a cousin of the eighth prime minister of Canada, Sir Robert Borden. CFB Borden is named after Frederick Borden.

1960
The federal government's Bill C-150 was passed, amending the criminal law and criminal procedure in Canada. Among a number of changes, it decriminalized homosexuality and allowed abortion under certain conditions, decriminalized the sale of contraceptives, and established the regulation of lotteries and rules on gun possession.

1756
Governor Charles Lawrence issued a bounty proclamation for scalps of Mi'kmaq warriors after the native raid on Lunenburg. Women and children were to be taken prisoner, not killed. (Also see, Mi'kmaq and Maliseet warriors... May 8, 1756.)

MAY 15TH

A View of Halifax in Nova Scotia from Cornwallis Island, with a Squadron Going Off to Louisbourg in the Year 1757, by Thomas Davies.

1754

The French and Indian War begins — later (1756) officially becoming The Seven Years' War between England and France. In Nova Scotia, it started with a series of conflicts in June of 1755, namely the Battle of Fort Beauséjour, with the deportation of the Acadians in the fall. By July 1757, there were in excess of 20,000 soldiers and sailors in Halifax with plans to attack the French at Louisbourg. Halifax had rapidly transformed from a small, insignificant seaport into a major military and naval base on the North Atlantic coast. Soon Army officer (and watercolour painter) Thomas Davies (1737–1812) would arrive with the fleet on July 9. He would paint a picture of this time called *A View of Halifax in Nova Scotia from Cornwallis Island, with a Squadron going off to Louisburg in the year 1757*. The squadron's effort failed and it wasn't until May of 1758 that another British attack was launched against Louisbourg. That time it succeeded.

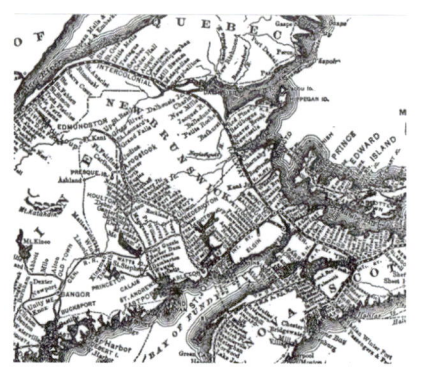

1851

Joseph Howe spoke to the idea of constructing an intercolonial railway at the Mason's Hall in Halifax. "I am neither a prophet, nor the son of a prophet, yet I will venture to predict that in five years we shall make the journey hence to Quebec and Montreal, and home through Portland and St. John, by rail; and I believe that many in this room will live to hear the whistle of the steam engine in the passes of the Rocky Mountains, and to make the journey from Halifax to the Pacific in five or six days." (Speech of the Hon. Joseph Howe)

Joseph Howe's vision eventually came true – a map of the Intercolonial Railway, 1877.

May 16th

1604

Pierre Dugua, sieur de Mons (de Monts), with Baron de Poutrincourt, Samuel de Champlain and their crew, sailed into what is now known as the Annapolis Basin. They later crossed the Baie Françoise (Bay of Fundy) and settled for their first winter on the island of St. Croix (located on what became the border between New Brunswick and eastern Maine). After much hardship, in the spring of 1605 they moved the settlement to Port Royale (now Annapolis Royal), and built and established the Habitation, the first permanent French settlement in what later became known as Canada. They established a close friendship with Mi'kmaq Grand Chief Membertou (Kjisaqmaw Maupeltuk) and the Mi'kmaq people. It is believed that the first black presence in Canada, in the person of Mathieu Da Costa (De Coste), had also accompanied them as an interpreter with the Indigenous peoples. As for Champlain, he had first sailed to North America with the French merchant Francois Gravé Du Pont, arriving at Tadoussac, Quebec, on March 15, 1603. He later returned to France and published an account of his journey titled *Des Sauvages, ou, voyage de Samuel Champlain, de Brouage, fait en la France nouvelle, l'an mil six cens trois* (Concerning the Savages: or, Travels of Samuel Champlain of Brouages, made in New France in the year 1603).

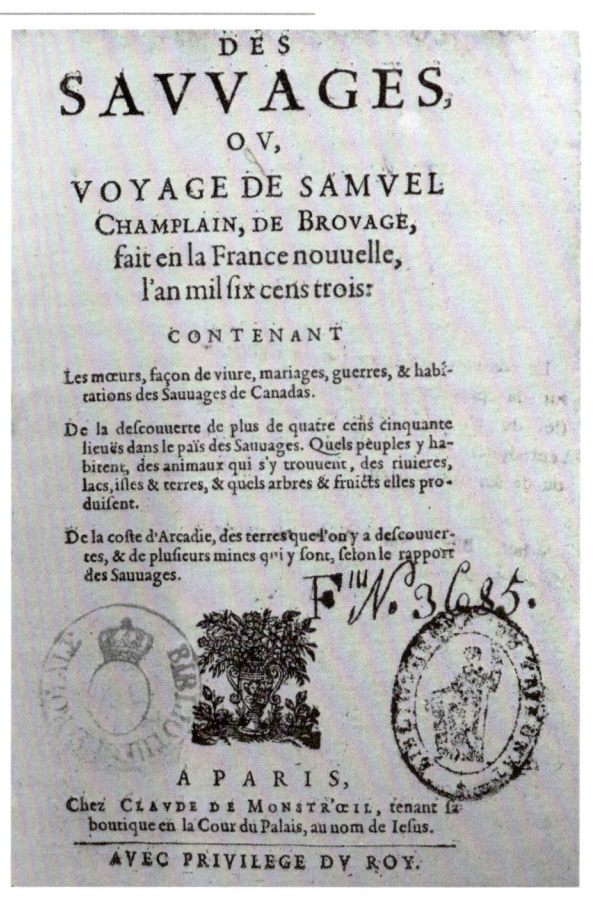

The title page of Champlain's book.

May 17th

1799

Edward, Duke of Kent, was made commander in chief of British Forces in North America. The duke had arrived in 1796 from St. Kitts to be commander of the garrison at Halifax.

May 18th

1850

A picture was taken of Molly Muise, Mi'kmaq elder, who lived to a great age at Annapolis Royal. It is considered one of the earliest portraits of a Mi'kmaw person by a photographic process.

Molly Muise.

May 19th

2006
DHX Media began trading as a public company on the Toronto Stock Exchange (TSX) — headquartered in Halifax, the company was formed as a merger between DECODE Entertainment and the Halifax Film Company, joining forces to be the leading children's and family entertainment program distributor, producer and co-producer. As of 2016, the company maintained one the world's largest independent libraries of children's and family content at more than 11,500 hours, with offices in fifteen cities worldwide. In May 2017, DHX Media made a $345 million dollar purchase for the controlling interest (80 per cent) in the *Charlie Brown/Peanuts* and *Strawberry Shortcake* (100 per cent) entertainment material for future development.

1995
Nova Scotia declared the Nova Scotia Duck Tolling Retriever to be the provincial dog.

The Nova Scotia Duck Tolling Retriever.

May 20th

2008
Pumpkin king Howard Dill died in Windsor (b. 1934). He was a legendary farmer and winner of largest pumpkin weigh-offs, as well as a world-renowned grower of giant gourds. Dill was also an avid hockey historian and enabled Windsor's claim to the title "Birthplace of Hockey." (Also see Garth Vaughan, September 1, 1996.)

Howard Dill.

May 21st

1992
From May 21 to 23, St. Francis Xavier University hosted the first annual conference of the Celtic Studies Association of North America. It was organized under the leadership of Ken Nilsen, the first chair of Gaelic Studies, and Sister Margaret MacDonell, retired chair of the Department of Celtic Studies. The endowment for the chair of Gaelic Studies is named in honour of Sister Saint Veronica (Mary MacDonald), who was a Gaelic-speaker and the first woman to be appointed to the St. Francis Xavier faculty (History, from 1937 to 1970). Sister Margaret MacDonell authored The *Emigrant Experience: Songs of Highland Emigrants in North America* (University of Toronto Press, 1982).

MAY 22ND

1611
First Jesuits arrived in Port Royal, Father Pierre Biard and Father Ennemond Masse. An earlier Jesuit mission had been established in 1609 on Penobscot Bay. In 1632–33, two Jesuits would also reside at St. Anne's Bay in Cape Breton. The Jesuit Order, known as the Society of Jesus, had been approved by Pope Paul III in 1540.

MAY 23RD

1916
The 85th Battalion (Nova Scotia Highlanders) was mobilized at Aldershot. They embarked for Great Britain on October 12.

MAY 24TH

The Royal Halifax Yacht Club, 1871.

James Wolfe by Joseph Highmore.

1861
The Halifax Yacht Club was renamed the Royal Halifax Yacht Club (and, later, again renamed the Royal Nova Scotia Yacht Squadron). The club was the oldest yacht club in North America having come into being on July 27, 1837. In 1860, as a nineteen-year-old, His Royal Highness Albert Edward, the Prince of Wales, later King Edward VII, had visited Halifax. An enthusiastic yachtsman, he participated in a regatta in his honour at the club. He later undertook to commission a cup, the Prince of Wales Cup, for the club. On this date in 1861, Queen Victoria gave permission to use the term "Royal" in the club's name.

1758
While in Halifax preparing for the British attack on Fortress Louisbourg, Brigadier General James Wolfe (age thirty-one) hosted a party for forty-seven of his men at the Great Pontack Inn (built prior to 1754, located at the corner of Duke and Water Streets). The event included ten musicians and plenty of food and liquid refreshments. Wolfe would return to the Pontack a year later on a stopover on his way to Quebec and the Battle of the Plains of Abraham.

May 25th

The Port Royal Settlement, by Francis Back.

1925
The Habitation at Port Royal was designated a National Historic Site by the Historic Sites and Monuments Board. It was established by France in 1605 as the first successful settlement in North America, serving as the capital of Acadia till its destruction by British military forces in 1613. A replica of the Habitation, based on Champlain's original plans, was constructed from 1939 to 1941 and was the first National Historic site to have a replica structure built.

May 26th

1989
Reverend William Pearly Oliver died (b. 1912). He was a leading African Nova Scotian who, with his wife, Pearleen Borden Oliver, was a strong advocate for social justice. A graduate of Acadia University (1934), and minister at Cornwallis Street Baptist Church (1937–1962), he was instrumental in developing many progressive organizations, including the Nova Scotia Association for the Advancement of Colored People (1945), the NS Human Rights Commission (1967), the Black United Front (1969), the Black Cultural Centre for Nova Scotia (1983) and supporting the case of Viola Desmond. He was awarded the Order of Canada in 1984.

May 27th

1945
On CBC Radio this day, Nora Bateson, the former Nova Scotia Director of Libraries (1938–1945), championed a vision of libraries as agents of personal and community development. It was twenty days after Germany had surrendered, and the VE Day riots had occurred earlier in the month in Halifax. A month earlier, Premier Macmillan had fired her when she had made a public remark that Nova Scotia was a "library desert."

Nora Bateson.

May 28th

1782
During the American Revolution, the Battle of Halifax took place between the American privateer *Jack* and the 14-gun Royal Naval brig HMS *Observer* off Halifax Harbour's Sambro Light. The *Jack* lost the battle, striking its colours the next day. The battle was one of several in the area.

The American privateer Jack *and the 14-gun Royal Navy brig HMS* Observer *engage in battle off Halifax Harbour's Sambro Light.*

May 29th

1852
George Wylie Hutchinson was born in Great Village, NS (d. 1942). He left the province as a young ship-cabin's boy. Later he studied art at the Royal Academy School in London (1880–1885). He became a noted painter and an illustrator in Britain, working for such publications as the *Illustrated London News*, as well as illustrating many works for authors who were at the centre of London literary circles — such as Arthur Conan Doyle, Rudyard Kipling, Robert Louis Stevenson and Israel Zangwill. Hutchinson was also the 'Great Uncle George' to the American poet Elizabeth Bishop (1911–1979). As historian Sandra Barry points out, Bishop had spent time in Great Village with her maternal grandparents, and some of her poems were influenced by Hutchinson paintings that hung in her grandparent's home.

George Wylie Hutchinson — self-portrait, 1914.

May 30th

1983
Symphony Nova Scotia (SNS) was created, beginning with thirteen full-time players for a January–May season, under the direction of conductor Boris Brott and board president Brian Flemming. In the past, orchestras had been formed in Halifax, beginning in 1897 with the Halifax Symphony Orchestra (disbanded in 1908). SNS grew to employ thirty-seven full-time musicians for a 33-week season under the direction of Bernhard Gueller.

May 31st

1820
Lord Dalhousie presented to the province portraits of George II (later proved to be of George I) and Queen Caroline, both received from his castle in Scotland.

1867
The Pictou Railway opened.

JUNE

June 1st

Jewish Legion, Fort Edward, Nova Scotia, Yom Kippur, 1918.

1918
Young recruit David Ben-Gurion (1886–1973) arrived in Windsor, NS, to begin training with the newly formed Jewish Legion of the British Army at Fort Edward, with a plan to fight against the Ottoman Turks in Palestine. Over 1,100 non-commissioned Jewish officers were trained in Windsor. Ben-Gurion had enlisted on April 26, 1918, in New York City. He would later become a primary founder of the State of Israel and its first prime minister.

The former CBC Radio building on the corner of Sackville and South Park streets, Halifax, Nova Scotia. It was torn down in 2016 to make way for condos.

1970
CBC *Information Morning Halifax* began broadcasting, featured co-hosts Bob Oxley and Paul Kells, news by Frank Cameron and Brian Bullock, sports by George Young and weather by Reid Dexter. The following year, Don Tremaine became a host with Gerry Fogarty as sportscaster. By 1976, Don Connolly joined Tremaine. The show went on later to feature Don Connolly, with co-host Louise Renault, sports by John Hancock and weather by Brennan Mitchell.

June 2nd

1820
Sir James Kempt (1765–1854) was sworn in as lieutenant governor. He served from 1820 to 1828, and was a veteran of the Battle of Waterloo and the War of 1812, amongst other military exploits. He also served as Governor of British North America (1828–1830). Kemptville and the Kempt Shore were named after him.

2008
The Truth and Reconciliation Commission of Canada was established to respond to the accusation of abuse and other ill effects on First Nations children that resulted from the Indian residential school program. After a series of national events and consultations, the commission concluded its work in June of 2015, submitting a report identifying ninety-four "Calls to Action' to 'redress the legacy of residential schools and advance the process of Canadian reconciliation."

Promotional material for the Apple Blossom Festival.

1933
The first Apple Blossom Festival was held in the Annapolis Valley.

June 3rd

1926
Flora MacDonald was born in North Sydney (d. 2015). A distinguished Canadian politician and humanitarian, she was first elected to the House of Commons in 1972. She was Canada's first female foreign minister and the first woman to seek the leadership of the Progressive Conservatives, in 1976.

1825
The schooner *Mary* began a mail packet and passenger service from Pictou to Charlottetown, PEI, every Tuesday evening. By 1832, a weekly service was being provided with the steamboat SS *Pocahontas*. By 1864, the paddle steamer SS *Princess of Wales* was providing regular service.

1858
The Windsor Branch of the Nova Scotia Railroad was opened to Windsor Junction and on to Halifax. To celebrate the opening of the Windsor Branch, the following Tuesday, June 8, was declared a public holiday in Halifax by the lieutenant governor, His Excellency Sir Gaspard le Marchant, the Earl of Mulgrave; all shops and offices were closed to enable the population to celebrate.

Flora MacDonald.

June 4th

Sketch of Melville Island, 1855, by Lieut. Bland, 76th Regiment (1827–1893) published in the London Illustrated News.

The Planters Monument.

1814
A captured American privateer and prisoner at Melville Island, Benjamin Franklin Palmer, wrote in his diary, "Four prisoners carried to Target Hill [later known as Deadman's Island] this morning, a place where they bury the dead. I'm fearful a number of us will visit that place this summer if not shortly released." It's estimated that, between 1812 and 1815, as many as 8,000 captured American soldiers, sailors and privateers were held at the Melville Island Prison. They are now remembered each year.

1760
The New England Planters began to arrive in Nova Scotia to settle on former Acadian lands. Townships were established in Newport, Falmouth and Horton. Many Planter descendants still reside in the area, some on the original land grants. One of their landing places was at Boudreau's Bank on the Rivière des Habitants (in Mi'kmaq, the Chijekwtook/Jijutu'kwejk). They later would rename the river and district Cornwallis.

1978
The Evelyn Richardson Non-Fiction Award was first awarded — named in honour of Evelyn Richardson (1902–1976), who won the Governor General's Non-Fiction Award in 1945 for *We Keep a Light,* her memoir of life as a family of lighthouse keepers in Shelburne County. As of 2017, the award had honoured the best non-fiction titles by Nova Scotian authors for thirty-nine years.

June 5th

1918
While the First World War raged on in Europe, by late spring 1918 the first phase of a "three day fever" began to appear. A few deaths were reported, while some victims (ages fifteen to forty) recovered after a few days. However, by September the virus appeared in North America and became widespread globally. It did not discriminate and struck fast, eluding treatment and control. It became known as the "Spanish Influenza." By 1919, it would sweep the world, killing an estimated 50 million people, one fifth of the world's population at that time (50,000 Canadians would die; 1,700 to 2,000 died in Nova Scotia). The influenza killed more people than any other illness in recorded history.

June 6th

HMS Shannon leading her prize, the American Frigate Chesapeake into Halifax Harbour, on the 6th June 1813, by J.G. Schetly.

1813

The victorious Royal Navy frigate HMS *Shannon* returned to Halifax under the command of Provo William Parry Wallis. In tow, he had the USS *Chesapeake* from Boston. Wallis's captain had died during the battle outside Boston Harbour on June 1. Wallis took command and sailed the *Shannon* back to Halifax with the captured *Chesapeake* in tow. *Chesapeake*'s commander, Captain James Lawrence, died of his wounds on the way to Halifax. He was buried with full military honours in St. Paul's Cemetery (now called the Old Burying Ground). But ten weeks later, his body, and that of his first lieutenant, Augustus Ludlow, who had also died during the battle, were disinterred and returned to the US where they were buried in the Trinity Churchyard in New York City. The remaining crew (320) were marched to the Melville Island Prison on the Northwest Arm. (Also see Sir Provo William Parry Wallis, April 12, 1791)

Halifax from George's Island, as portrayed by G.I. Parkyns in 1801, just after the time William Cobbett visited the town.

1800

William Cobbett (1763–1835) and family arrived in Halifax, fleeing from the United States en route to England. He had served with the 54th Regiment of Foot in New Brunswick, became a popular writer (author of *The Soldier's Friend* in 1792), and was an early witness to the French Revolution. But he had also become a controversial political and pro-British pamphleteer and commentator in the United States. He had been charged there with defamation by Dr. Benjamin Rush, an eminent physician, and now was in flight. Back in Britain, he became a publisher and a strong voice for parliamentary reform.

June 7th

1861
Annie Louise Prat was born in Paradise, Annapolis County. Her life spanned a century. She was the daughter of Samuel Prat and Elizabeth (née Morse). Annie and her siblings were raised in Wolfville where her father was the first train-station master, and later became the superintendent of several stations in the Annapolis Valley. Her mother was the sister of John Morse, founder of Morse's Tea in Halifax. Annie became a professional artist, studying at the School of the Art Institute of Chicago in 1896, while her sister Minnie studied in New York, becoming North America's first fully-qualified woman bookbinder. Her younger sister, May Rosina, joined Minnie in NY to study leatherwork, and they later ran a successful bookbinding and leather studio in the city. Tragically, in 1901 at age thirty-three, Minnie died as a result of typhoid fever. May eventually returned to Nova Scotia and married. Annie returned to NS, continuing her career as a semi-professional artist.

Annie L. Prat, 1885, Parkinson, NY.

1995
Charles S.A. Ritchie died (b. 1906 in Halifax). Educated at King's College, and later at Oxford, Harvard and the École Libre des Sciences Politiques, he became a distinguished Canadian diplomat and a compelling diarist. He won the 1974 Governor General's Award for his diary account published in 1974 as *The Siren Years: A Canadian Diplomat Abroad 1937–1945*. He later published three further volumes: *An Appetite for Life* (1977), *Diplomatic Passport* (1981), and *Storm Signals* (1983).

1753
Fourteen hundred German settlers, who had arrived in 1750–51, left Halifax to establish a settlement in Lunenburg.

June 8th

2013
Former CBC producer Nicholas 'Manny' Pittson died (b. Halifax, 1937). He had a career spanning sixty years. He started in high school as an announcer at CHNS Radio in Halifax, later becoming the youngest producer in Canada at CBC Halifax, where he produced *Frank's Bandstand*, *Take Thirty* and *Singalong Jubilee*, and launched the careers of many iconic Canadian singers. As an independent producer, he brought such shows as *Don Messer's Jubilee* and *Ryan's Fancy* to CHCH Hamilton. (Also see *Singalong Jubilee*, July 3, 1961.)

Manny Pittson.

June 8th (cont'd)

1755

Admiral Edward Boscawen (1711–1761) engaged a French fleet in the Newfoundland fog and, in capturing the sixty-four-gun *Alcide* (and the *Lys*), discovered a specific piece of intelligence. Among the French Admiral Hocquart's papers was a document relating how French troops, working in concert with a general Acadian-Indian uprising, planned to pit some 8,000 men against 3,000 British in an attempt to attack Halifax. Thousands of scalping knives were also found packed into the ships' holds. Also onboard the *Alcide* was Francois-Pierre de Rigaud de Vaudreuil, governor of Trois-Rivières (returning from France). He was taken as a prisoner to Halifax. While in prison, Vaudreuil met another prisoner, acting as a British spy, named Thomas Pichon. Unsuspecting, Vaudreuil shared a map and French plans for seizing Halifax with Pichon. The information was passed on.

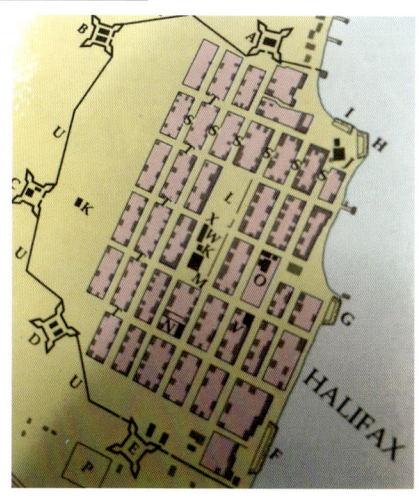

A rendition of a map and directory of the Halifax settlement that François-Pierre de Rigaud de Vaudreuil had passed on to Thomas Pichon. 1755.

June 9th

1975

Jane Barnes Wisdom died in Pictou County at the age of ninety-one (b. 1884). Born in New Brunswick, she had studied social work in New York and came to Halifax in 1916 to work with the Halifax Welfare Bureau. Considered the first professional social worker in Nova Scotia, she survived the Halifax Explosion and played an active role in the recovery efforts. She did research on the working conditions of women in Nova Scotia in 1920, and in the early forties she conducted studies on the social conditions in the coal mining town of Glace Bay with a colleague, Charlotte Whitton (who later became mayor of Ottawa). She subsequently developed the social services program for Glace Bay and served as their first welfare officer, retiring from that role in 1952.

2013

The Lost at Sea Memorial monument was unveiled on Water Street in Yarmouth to commemorate all the sons and daughters of Yarmouth County who died at sea. For example, in the year 1879 alone no fewer than thirty-one vessels were lost along with 106 persons.

1993

Gordon Parsons died (age forty-two). He was an eclectic cinephile and writer, and a driving force in the Atlantic Canada film industry, including the founding of Wormwood's Dog and Monkey Cinema (1976). In 1991 he became the Executive Director of the Atlantic Film Festival (which began in St. John's, NL). Wormwood closed in 1998.

June 10th

1892

Charles Fenery died (b. Upper Sackville, January 1821). He was the inventor of paper from wood pulp and a poet.

June 11th

A photographer taking a picture of the last tram that ran in Halifax, on March 26, 1949.

1866
The Halifax Street Railway Company was established by William O'Brien, consisting of five horse-drawn vehicles providing passenger transit service in the city. Through various organizational changes and expansions, the horse-drawn vehicles continued till May 31, 1896, when the Halifax Electric Tramway Company began operating streetcars. In 1949, the system changed over to electric trolley coaches and then later to gas-powered buses. By January 1, 1970, the City of Halifax was managing the operation. By January 2014, the service was called Halifax Transit and it included the Dartmouth ferry services (started in 1752), and 312 buses on 57 bus routes. In 2016 bus ridership was over 4 million.

By Lawren Harris, from his visit to report on the miner's strike in 1925. Miner's Houses, 1925.

1925
Group of Seven founding artist Lawren Harris (1885–1970) was in the Glace Bay–New Waterford area reporting on the miner's strike on a commission from the *Toronto Star*. Ten years earlier, he had been on the battlefields of Europe. During his time in Cape Breton he produced somber images from what he witnessed, one being *Miner's Houses*. Earlier in the spring of 1921, Harris had also been in Halifax on his way to Newfoundland. He painted two specific works — *Elevator Court* and *Black Court*. (Also see Returning war artist. . .A.Y. Jackson, February 3, 1919.)

June 12th

2010
A ceremony attended by approximately 400 people, including American Civil War reenactment soldiers, was held at Benjamin Jackson's grave site, marking it with a commemorative stone. Jackson (1835–1915) was a decorated American Civil War soldier, and a sailor, farmer and African Nova Scotian. He was born in Lochartville (near Hantsport).

Ben Jackson (1835–1915), a decorated American Civil War soldier, sailor, farmer and African Nova Scotian.

June 13th

1972

Natalie MacMaster was born in Troy, Inverness County, Cape Breton. She began playing the fiddle at the age of nine and her musical career at sixteen. By 2017 the award-winning fiddler had created twelve albums and toured extensively with many international artists. She won numerous musical awards and was made a member of the Order of Canada in 2006. Her uncle was the late renowned Cape Breton fiddler Buddy MacMaster (see August 20, 2014) and she married fellow fiddler Donnell Leahy. Their children were destined to become the next generation of fiddle players.

Natalie MacMaster.

June 14th

2012

Nova Scotia writer, editor and author Scott Milsom died. He was a co-founder and editor of the award-winning *New Maritimes* quarterly journal. He was also author of *Voices of Nova Scotia Community: A Written Democracy* (Fernwood, 2003), which explored why the people of small communities across Nova Scotia value the quality of life they enjoy.

June 15th

2016

The $150-million dollar Big Lift project on the sixty-year-old Angus L. Macdonald Bridge in Halifax officially reached its halfway point in the work to replace all the deck segments of the bridge. By this date, the contractor, the American Bridge Canada Company, had replaced twenty segments out of a total of forty-six, with plans to complete the deck replacement by spring 2017.

The Big Lift neared structural completion in February, 2017.

June 16th

1874
William A. White was born in Virginia to two former slaves. He became the second graduate of African descent from Acadia University (1903). He later became a chaplain and the first black officer serving in the entire British Army during the First World War. He was the father of Portia White, as well as politicians Bill and Jack White. He was the first Canadian black person to be given an honorary doctorate (from Acadia University), in 1936.

Rev. William A. White.

June 17th

Gaspereau Winery, Annapolis Valley.

2017
The National Wine Awards were hosted in Greenwich, Nova Scotia. Featuring over 1,700 wines and ciders, it was the largest wine awards event in Canadian history, featuring six tables of judges. The event was also hosted in Nova Scotia in 2011. The Winery Association of Nova Scotia indicated that, as of 2017, there were seventy grape growers and more than 800 acres under vine in various regions across Nova Scotia, with eleven wineries in operation.

June 18th

1784
The final decision was made in Britain to separate Nova Scotia and New Brunswick.

1906
British imperial government properties in Halifax were handed over to the Dominion.

June 19th

1849
James Burns Barry, Jr. (1819–1906) of Pictou published his diary — the first of five volumes. An accomplished fiddle player and composer, as well as a piper, artist and printer of some renown (on a press he built himself), he also compiled two volumes of music, consisting of 2,248 tunes, which were later housed at the NS Archives.

June 20th

1833
The *Maid of the Mist* steamboat made her first trip from Saint John to Windsor.

June 21st

1749
After making their passage across the ocean in thirteen transports and one sloop-of-war (the *Sphinx*), Colonel Edward Cornwallis (age thirty-six) and 2,547 volunteer settlers and soldiers arrived at what later became Halifax, and was then called Chebucto by the British, Cheboutou by the French and K'jipuktuk by the Mi'kmaq, meaning chief of biggest harbour. Their purpose was to establish a new state-sponsored settlement in British North America. The settlers included 1,174 families (with 440 children) who were from released army and navy personnel. The contingent also included active soldiers to protect the settlement and 420 "servants." The date of arrival on the June 21 was based on the Julian Calendar — it would be July 2nd in our modern Gregorian calendar. (The Julian calendar changed to Gregorian on January 1, 1752.). Upon establishing the settlement on the west side of the harbour, Cornwallis named it *Halifax*, after the Earl of Halifax, George Montagu-Dunk, who was the president of the Board of Trade and Plantations, the body that had proposed the settlement, which had earlier been encouraged by New England Massachusetts Governor William Shirley, who saw it as a British priority in providing security to the northern colonies as a counterbalance to Louisbourg. Cornwallis reaffirmed British adherence to the 1726 Peace and Friendship Treaty agreements in a meeting with some Maliseet and Mi'kmaq chiefs in August. Not all accepted this new British occupation of their territory and in September a number of Mi'kmaq Chiefs expressed their opposition to the Halifax settlement in a letter to Cornwallis and warned that it could be attacked as a violation of the treaty agreements.

Colonel Edward Cornwallis of the 24th Regt. of Foot *by Sir George Chalmers, 1755.*

June 22nd

1897
Queen Victoria's Diamond Jubilee Holiday took place in Halifax with a military review on the Commons, watched by some 25,000. There were large displays of rockets, marching tattoos, ceremonies and music.

June 23rd

1930
The CN-owned Nova Scotian Hotel opened in Halifax, boasting 130 rooms, five suites and a ballroom that could accommodate up to 275 guests. CN sold it in 1981 and it became the Westin Nova Scotian.

June 24th

1497
Giovanni Caboto (John Cabot), an Italian navigator from Venice, who had sailed from England under the authority of Henry VII with a crew of eighteen in the *Matthew*, is said to have planted the British flag on Cape North, Cape Breton.

1911
Portia White was born in Truro (d. 1968). She was the first black Canadian operatic contralto concert singer to win international acclaim, making her national debut as a singer in Toronto in 1941. The Portia White Prize was named in her honour. (Also See William A. White, June 16, 1874.)

A replica of John Cabot's ship and sail.

Portia White.

June 25th

1761

The Burying the Hatchet Ceremony (also known as the Governor's Farm Ceremony — at the Spring Garden Road location of the Halifax Provincial Court House) took place with Mi'kmaq chiefs and colonial officials ended a period of protracted warfare that had lasted over seventy-five years between the Mi'kmaq/French alliance and the British. The French missionary Abbé Pierre Maillard acted as interpreter.

June 26th

The Halifax and Pictou Coach En Route, 1857. *Gaspard LeMarchant Tupper.*

1854

World travel writer Isabella Lucy Bird (1831–1904) arrived in Halifax on the Cunard Royal Mail steamship the *Canada*, just in from Liverpool, England, after a nine-day voyage. Bird was travelling with her cousins from PEI (the Swabeys) who had been visiting in London. After a two-day stay in Halifax they left at 6 p.m. by stagecoach to Truro, then on to Pictou to catch a steamer to Charlottetown. Bird would stay in PEI for six weeks before leaving on a steamer, and then a train for Boston. Over the summer and early fall she visited Cincinnati, Chicago, Toronto, Hamilton, Niagara Falls, Montreal, Quebec, New York and Boston. From there she returned to England on the Cunard steamship *America*, stopping off once again in Halifax on November 22. In 1892, she would be the first woman to be elected Fellow of the Royal Geographical Society, and in 1897 the Royal Photographic Society.

Isabella Lucy Bird.

June 27th

2013
Spoken word artist, activist and educator El Jones was announced Halifax Regional Municipality's poet laureate for 2013–2015. Previous poet laureates for HRM included Tanya Davis (2011–2012), Shauntay Grant (2009–2011), Lorri Neilsen Glenn (2005–2009) and inaugural poet laureate Sue MacLeod (2001–2005). Following El Jones was Rebecca Thomas (2016–2018).

1984
The Metro Food Bank Society began in Halifax (later Feed Nova Scotia). The society grew into a provincial operation and supported over 148 food banks, distributing food and providing referrals to community services across the province for families in need. In 2017, over 19,722 Nova Scotians turned to food banks each month.

El Jones.

June 28th

1794
Prince Edward, Duke of Kent and Strathearn (1767–1820), fourth son of King George III, arrived (aged twenty-seven) in Halifax as commander of the troops in Nova Scotia and New Brunswick (from 1794 till 1800). He was the first member of the royal family to live in North America for more than a short visit. The prince was offered the rural estate of Lieutenant Governor Sir John Wentworth as his residence. The prince liked it so much he renovated and expanded the estate (later known as the Hemlock Ravine Park). All that would remain of the original estate was the music room (rotunda), a small, round room built on a knoll overlooking the Bedford Basin. Upon his return to England, the prince became the father of the future Queen Victoria.

Music House, Prince's Lodge, by William Eagar, 1839.

June 29th

1749

The new French governor of Île Royale (the future Cape Breton), Charles des Herbiers de LaRalière (1700–1752), arrived in Louisbourg with two eighty-gun ships and twenty transports, with 2,000 returning French civilians and 1,000 soldiers. Under the terms of the Treaty of Aix-la-Chapelle (1748), Louisbourg had been returned to the French. The British commander on site, Peregrine Thomas Hopson (1685–1759), handed the keys over to des Herbiers. In late July, the French and their transports assisted in moving Hopson and his troops to Halifax where Governor Cornwallis had just begun to establish a British settlement (also see June 21, 1749). Des Herbiers would return to France in 1751, being replaced by Governor Jean-Louis, Comte de Raymond (1702–1771).

2011

The Bras d'Or Lake Biosphere Reserve, located on Cape Breton Island, was designated a UNESCO Biosphere Reserve. As part of a world network for promoting exchange of information, experience and personnel. As of 2017 there were 621 biosphere reserve sites in 117 countries. Sixteen of those being in Canada.

June 30th

Grand Pré National Historic Site.

2012

The National Historic Site and surrounding landscape of Grand Pré was given a UNESCO World Heritage designation, qualifying under the cultural landscape category. The Grand Pré area encompassed 1,300 hectares of land and properties in Nova Scotia's Annapolis Valley. It was the centre of French Acadian settlement from 1682 to 1755. The National Historic Site honours the deportation of the Acadians, which began in 1755 and continued until 1762.

July

July 1st

Hole 12 of the Cape Breton Highland Golf Links, which opened in 1941.

1941

The Cape Breton Highland Links golf course in Ingonish opened. Designed by golf course architect Stanley W. Thompson (1893–1953), it was recognized as one of his masterpieces — one of 145 courses he designed from Cape Breton to Brazil. "Thompson gave every hole a Gaelic name and the fourth has an appropriate one – Heich O' Fash. That translates as Heap of Trouble," wrote Bob Weeks.

1867

As proclaimed by Queen Victoria, four provinces were joined as "One dominion under the name of Canada . . . with a Constitution similar in Principle to that of the United Kingdom": Canada West (formerly Upper Canada, then Ontario), Canada East (formerly Lower Canada, later Quebec), Nova Scotia and New Brunswick. Title to the Northwest Territories was transferred by the Hudson's Bay Company in 1870, and the province of Manitoba joined (the first to be established by the Parliament of Canada). British Columbia joined Confederation in 1871, followed by Prince Edward Island in 1873. The Yukon Territory was created by Parliament in 1898, followed by Alberta and Saskatchewan in 1905. The Dominion of Newfoundland (later Newfoundland and Labrador), Britain's oldest colony in the Americas, joined Canada as a province in 1949. Nunavut was created in 1999. As the first prime minister, Sir John A. Macdonald formed the first government of the Dominion of Canada. As of 2017, there were 338 Members of Parliament and 105 Senators.

July 2nd

1821
Sir Charles Tupper was born in Amherst. He was educated at Horton Academy became a doctor and later was an MLA and served as premier of Nova Scotia. He was become the last surviving Father of Confederation, a federal cabinet member, the sixth prime minister of Canada, and a commissioner to London. He published *Recollections of Sixty Years* in 1914. He died in England in 1915 and was interred at the St. John's Cemetery in Halifax.

Charles Tupper.

July 3rd

1961
CBC television began broadcasting *Singalong Jubilee* (1961–1974). It started as a summer replacement for the popular *Don Messer Show*. *Singalong Jubilee* was produced by Manny Pittson, with co-producer and host Bill Langstroth, singer Jim Bennett and Brian Ahern as the music director. The program featured musical performances by local singers in a variety of music genres, such as Anne Murray, Catherine McKinnon, Gene MacLellan, Edith Butler and many more who gained attention from their appearances. (Also see Anne Murray, February 15, 1979.)

Bill Langestroth with the cast of Singalong Jubilee.

July 4th

1940
Haliburton Museum opened in Windsor. Formerly known as the Clifton House, the former residence of noted nineteenth century author and judge Thomas Chandler Haliburton was constructed in 1837. He lived there with his wife, Louisa Neville, and their seven children (three had died in their first years) till he was widowed in 1841. He moved to England in 1856. Now known as the Haliburton House, it was the first Historic House Museum in Nova Scotia.

400 YEARS IN 365 DAYS

July 5th

1890
Catherine Susan Ann Howe (née McNab) died. Born in St. John's, Newfoundland, in 1807, she moved to Halifax in 1817 and lived with her parents on McNab's Island. On February 3, 1828, at St. Paul's Church, she married Joseph Howe. She helped run his business as well as their busy household and family. She was buried in Camp Hill Cemetery.

1775
Governor Francis Legge issued a *Proclamation forbidding persons to Aid or Correspond with any persons in [American] Rebellion*. Justices of the peace were directed to proclaim it and "cause it to be read several times in all places of public worship." Seventy-five per cent of Nova Scotia's settler population of 20,000 was of New England origin.

July 6th

1921
Allan J. MacEachen was born in Inverness, Cape Breton Island. He entered politics in 1953 as an MP for Inverness-Richmond (1953–'58, 1962–'68) and for Cape Breton Highlands–Canso (1968–'84). He served in several portfolios, including as deputy prime minister under Pierre Elliott Trudeau, from 1977 to 1979. He was later appointed to the Senate.

Allan J. MacEachen.

July 7th

Covenanter's Church, Grand Pré, the oldest extant Presbyterian Church in Canada — constructed between 1804 and 1811.

1795
The first meeting of Presbyterian Synod occurred near Alma, Pictou County.

Cliffs and reefs at low tide at Joggins, Nova Scotia.

2008
The Joggins Fossil Cliffs were named a UNESCO World Heritage Site, spanning more than fifteen kilometres of fossil-bearing cliffs that are witness to more than 310 million years of geological and paleontological riches. Across the Minas Basin from Joggins, in the rocks at Horton Bluff, Sir William Edmond Logan became the first to recognize in North America the tracks of Carboniferous vertebrate animals, in 1841.

July 8th

Nova Scotia artist Earl Bailly met Her Royal Highness Princess Elizabeth, 1951.

1903
Evern 'Earl' Bailly was born in Lunenburg (d. 1977). He contracted polio at age three and became a wheelchair-bound quadriplegic for the rest of his life. However, by the age of six he learned to paint by holding a brush between his teeth and later became a highly-regarded artist. In 1947, he was featured in the film *On the Shores of Nova Scotia*.

Seascape, N.S., by *Earl Bailly.*

400 YEARS IN 365 DAYS

July 9th

Some members of the No. 2 Construction Battalion formed on July 5, 1916, Canada's first and only black battalion.

2016
A hundredth anniversary commemoration ceremony for the No. 2 Construction Battalion (formed on July 5, 1916), Canada's first and only black battalion was held at the deCoste Centre, Pictou. Over 500 members of the Nova Scotia black community volunteered for service with No. 2 Construction Battalion, and the unit also included 165 African Americans, along with volunteers from the British West Indies and Guyana. Before proceeding to France, the unit was 300 men understrength and was reorganized as a reinforced Construction Company of 10 officers and 506 men. In addition to No. 2 Construction Battalion, over 1,500 African Canadians served in other units of the Canadian Expeditionary Force, including 400 in infantry battalions.

July 10th

1970
The A. Murray MacKay Bridge over Halifax Harbour was officially opened. The bridge was named after Alexander Murray MacKay, who was chairman of the Halifax-Dartmouth Bridge Commission from 1951 to 1971. He had also overseen the construction of the Angus L. Macdonald Bridge.

The A. Murray MacKay Bridge.

July 11th

2009
Ex-Beatle Paul McCartney performed an outdoor concert on the Halifax Common. Though enjoyed immensely by those in attendance, ticket sales were less than anticipated and later a controversy unfolded when it was revealed that massive expenses associated with the concert had been underwritten with taxpayer funds.

1970
The Ross Farm Museum was formally opened by Premier G. I. Smith. Depicting life as it once was in rural Nova Scotia, it was named after Captain William Ross, who settled in the New Ross area in 1816.

July 12th

1625
Charles I renewed the 1621 royal charter first established by King James for the lands of New Scotland to Sir William Alexander, Earl of Stirling (1577–1640). The lands were known as Nova Scotia in Latin, Nouvelle Écosse in French and Alba Nuadh in Scottish Gaelic. The Royal Charter did not recognize Mi'kma'ki.

Sir William Alexander's New Scot Lande map, 1624.

July 13th

2009
Mi'kmaw basket-maker and Second World War veteran Noel Abraham 'Abe' Smith died at age ninety-two in Windsor (b. in Berwick, 1917). In 1991, he was featured with his wife, Rita, in a National Film Board film called *Kwa'nu'te* that profiled the artistry and skill of their basket-making. Rita (1918–1996) was the past president of the former Mi'kmaq Arts and Crafts Society, and was the first chief of Horton Mi'kmaw community (1984) — later known as Glooscap. She was also a founding Chief of the Confederacy of Mainland Mi'kmaq.

July 14th

1749
Governor Edward Cornwallis held his first council deliberations onboard the *Beaufort* transport in Halifax Harbour. On June 21, he had arrived in Chebouctou harbour with 2,547 volunteer settlers and soldiers. He had orders to establish and secure a settlement. At the council meeting, Governor Cornwallis opened his commission and took the oaths of office in the council's presence and the Civil Government was organized.

Table used by Edward Cornwallis on the ship Beaufort *to hold his first Nova Scotia Council meeting in 1749, now in the Red Chamber of the Nova Scotia Legislature building.*

July 15th

1872
Mary Eliza Herbert died (b. 1832). She was an author, poet and magazine editor as well as the first woman in Nova Scotia to edit and publish a magazine (at the age of eighteen): the *Mayflower*, or *Ladies' Acadian Newspaper*, a small thirty-two-page volume (1851–52). Her older sister was author, publisher and educator Sarah Herbert (1824–1846).

July 16th

Alex Colville Ocean Limited *1962 Oil and synthetic resin on hardboard Copyright A.C.Fine Art Inc.*

2013
Alex Colville died (b. 1920). An internationally renowned Canadian painter and Wolfville resident (from 1973), he was a Companion of the Order of Canada (1982), a recipient of the Order of Nova Scotia (2003) and appointed to the Privy Council (2003). In the summer of 2014 the Art Gallery of Ontario hosted Colville's work, one of the largest (more than 100 works) and most successful exhibits of an artist's work in its history.

1861
Richard Preston died (b. 1791). He was a religious leader (ordained on May 19, 1832) and abolitionist. He escaped slavery in Virginia to become an important leader for the African Nova Scotian community and in the international struggle against slavery (the community of Preston, NS, was named after him). He was the founder of the Cornwallis Street United Baptist Church in 1832.

Richard Preston.

July 17th

Engraving in the Illustrated London News *of the inauguration of the Welsford-Parker Monument in Halifax, June 17, 1860.*

1860
The unveiling of the Welsford-Parker Monument took place in St. Paul's Cemetery in Halifax. The monument was shaped in the form of a triumphal arch and surmounted by the British lion. It was built in memory of Major Augustus Frederick Welsford (1811–1855) and fellow soldier William Buck Carthew Augustus Parker (1823–1855) — commemorated as imperial heroes at the Battle of the Great Redan during the Siege of Sevastopol in Crimea. This monument became the fourth-oldest in Canada, and the only monument to the Crimean War (1853–February 1856) in North America.

July 18th

1912
The first Montessori School in North America opened in Baddeck. It began with the support of Alexander Graham Bell and his wife Mabel, for their grandchildren. Twelve pupils attended the school (in a loft of a Beinn Bhreagh warehouse) under the teaching direction of Roberta Fletcher from Washington.

July 19th

1784
The wooden frame of St. Peter's Roman Catholic Church was raised in Halifax at the corner of Spring Garden Road and Barrington. In 1833 the name was changed to St. Mary's Cathedral.

Roman Catholic Archdiocese of Halifax.

July 20th

1996
The National Historic Sites and Monuments Board unveiled a monument in honour of the memory of Black Loyalists who arrived in Birchtown, Shelburne County. Two smaller groups of Black Loyalists had also settled in Brindley town (present day Jordantown, Digby County) and Tracadie.

July 21st

1819
Richard Uniacke, Jr. fatally wounded Scottish merchant William Bowie in a duel on the Governor's North Farm (later known as the Fort Needham/Mulgrave Park area). The challenge occurred from insulting remarks made by Uniacke. Uniacke was charged with murder, but later found innocent.

July 22nd

Sandford Fleming (in tallest hat, near centre of photo) at the ceremony when the "Last Spike" was driven on the Canadian Pacific Railway, at Craigellachie, BC, November 7, 1885.

1915
Sir Sandford Fleming died in Halifax at his daughter's home. Born in Scotland in 1827, he came to Canada in 1845 with his family. He was Canada's foremost railway construction engineer for most of the Intercolonial Railway and the Canadian Pacific Railway, as well as an inventor and scientist who developed the model for international standard time. He was a founding member of the Royal Society of Canada, the Royal Canadian Institute and designed Canada's first official postage stamp — the Three-Pence Beaver. Fleming maintained a home in Halifax (having moved there in 1864 to oversee the building of the Intercolonial Railway to Nova Scotia). He first resided at 2549–2553 Brunswick Street and later on the Northwest Arm at Blenheim Cottage, where he retired. Before his death, he deeded 38 hectares of his cottage land to the city in 1908 — known as the Sir Sandford Fleming Park (or more popularly called Dingle Park). He was buried in the Beechwood Cemetery, Ottawa. (Also see George Munro Grant, December 22, 1835.)

July 23rd

1962
Daniel MacIvor, a well-known Canadian actor, playwright, screenwriter, film and theatre director, was born in Sydney. He won notable awards, including (twice) the Chalmers Award for best new Canadian play (twice), the 2006 Governor General's Award for Drama and the 2008 Siminovitch Prize in theatre (playwright). He held the position of Wester University's writer-in-residence for 2017-2018.

July 24th

Bluenose II, in Halifax Harbour.

1963
The *Bluenose II* launched in Lunenburg. A replica of the original *Bluenose*, it was built by Smith and Rhuland and sponsored by the Oland's Brewery (it was sold to the NS government in 1971). In 2009, the Nova Scotia government decided to restore the fifty-year-old *Bluenose II*. After lengthy delays, the ship was relaunched in 2015. An initial cost estimate of $14.4 million was budgeted for the restoration, but due to correcting a poor steering system, by 2017 it was reported that this cost had reached $25 million, plus $1 million to fight a design copyright issue, which was ultimately settled out of court.

Carrie Best postage stamp, Canada: 59 cents. Date of issue, 1 February 2011.

2001
Dr. Carrie Best died in New Glasgow (b. in Halifax, 1903). A journalist, radio broadcaster, social activist, author and respected leader of the African-Nova Scotian community, she founded (with her son, James C. Best) the first African-Nova Scotian–owned newspaper, the *Clarion*. The paper, which began publishing in 1946, was renamed in 1949 the *Negro Citizen* and continued until 1956. In her first issue, December 1946, Best broke the story of Viola Desmond's arrest and refusal to relinquish her seat in a "whites-only" section at the Roseland cinema in New Glasgow. (Also see Desmond, February 7, 1965.)

July 25th

1749
A Halifax settler, who arrived with Cornwallis's fleet in June, wrote to a friend back in Britain. The letter appeared in a periodical in October. Once established, a third of the settlers who arrived with Cornwallis either did not survive their first winter, or left for Boston.

July 26th

1939
The Gaelic College / Colaisde na Gàidhlig at St. Ann's opened. It was founded by Presbyterian minister A.W.R. MacKenzie. On December 6, 2012, the college was honoured by Her Majesty Queen Elizabeth II with the prefix Royal, as part of the college's seventy-fifth year of operation in promoting and preserving the customs and traditions of immigrants from the Highlands of Scotland.

July 27th

1758
With the surrender by French Governor Drucour, Major General Jeffery Amherst, with naval commander Admiral Edward Boscawen and Brigadiers James Wolfe, Charles Lawrence and Edward Whitmore, captured Fortress Louisburg. This was also the last major battle the Mi'kmaq fought against the British. (Also see Admiral Edward Boscawen, May 9, 1758.)

A View of Louisburg in North America, Taken from the Lighthouse, when that City was Besieged in 1758, Pierre Charles Canot, c. 1710–1777.

July 28th

1870
On July 28, 1870, Mather Byles Almon, president of the Bank of Nova Scotia, announced that the cashier, James Forman," . . . has been guilty of making many fraudulent entries in the books of the bank, by which he has abstracted a large amount of its funds." Forman was later accused of embezzling over $300,000 from the bank. Resigning in disgrace, Forman soon left Nova Scotia for England.

July 29th

2013
Well-known human rights crusader, lawyer and advocate for Nova Scotia's black community for over four decades, Burnley 'Rocky' Jones, died (b. 1941). "When you stick you head in the lion's mouth and hear him roar, there is no more excitement in this world of politics. It is the politics of survival for your community and change in your community" (*Burnley 'Rocky' Jones Revolutionary*, p. 212). In September 2016, an autobiography/memoir, *Burnley 'Rocky' Jones Revolutionary*, authored by Jones and James W. St. G. Walker, was published by Fernwood Publishing.

July 30th

1970
Maud Lewis died in Digby (b. 1903). She was one of Canada's best known and most prolific folk artists. The house she and her husband, Everett Lewis, lived in (and where she painted), was later installed as part of a permanent Maud Lewis exhibit in the care of the Art Gallery of Nova Scotia. Maude Lewis's life has been the subject of a documentary and stage play. In 2017 a feature film on her life, called *Maudie*, was released, starring Sally Hawkins as Maud Lewis, and Ethan Hawke as her husband, Everett.

Painting by Maud Lewis. The Art Gallery of Nova Scotia houses a permanent exhibit of her work.

July 31st

1967
The Cape Breton Miners' Museum at Glace Bay was officially opened. Prominent community leader and philanthropist Nina Cohen unveiled the cornerstone for the museum. She was instrumental in founding the Men of the Deeps choir in the summer of 1966. (Also see Nina Cohen, March 8, 1991.)

Nina Cohen unveiling the cornerstone of the Cape Breton Miners' Museum during the opening ceremonies July 31, 1967.

1885
Lumber baron B.B. Barnhill attempted to launch a great log raft at Joggins, bound for New York, but the attempt failed. In December 1887 a second raft was successfully launched, but it never made it to New York, as its tow line snapped in a storm along the Eastern Seaboard and the raft was lost. A third attempt was successful, but no further rafts were shipped from the Joggins Shore.

A great log raft.

AUGUST

August 1st

2010

Mi'kmaq First Nations celebrated the four hundredth anniversary of St. Anne's Mission at their annual gathering at Potlotek (Chapel Island) Cape Breton — one of the oldest Roman Catholic sites in Canada and recognized as a place of national historic significance. Saint Anne has been the recognised Mi'kmaq patron saint since 1629–30. It was also four hundred years since the baptism of Mi'kmaq Chief Membertou in 1610. But Potlotek is considered a sacred site beyond the Christian context, because it held significant historical and cultural meanings in Mi'kmaq history.

Chapel Island, Cape Breton.

August 2nd

1922

Alexander Graham Bell died in Baddeck. "Bell died of complications arising from diabetes . . . at his private estate, Beinn Bhreagh, Nova Scotia, at age 75 . . . [He] was buried atop Beinn Bhreagh mountain, where he had resided increasingly for the last 35 years of his life, overlooking Bras d'Or Lake. He was survived by his wife Mabel, his two daughters, Elsie May and Marian, and nine of his grandchildren." The Bell family had first come to summer at Baddeck in 1885 and later built their residence there, where Bell researched and conducted scientific experiments. (Also see First controlled flight, February 23, 1909.)

Alexander Graham Bell burial at his much-loved Beinn Bhreagh near Baddeck, Cape Breton.

August 3rd

1938
Nellie L. McClung (1873–1951), Canadian feminist, politician, author and social activist, wrote a piece in the *Register* (Town of Berwick), entitled *The Flavour of Nova Scotia*. She reflected upon visiting Nova Scotia to attend the Silver Jubilee Convention of the Women's Institutes of Nova Scotia in Halifax.

Nellie McClung.

1752
Thomas Peregrine Hopson replaced Governor Edward Cornwallis. Hopson had been sent from Gibraltar to reinforce the Louisbourg garrison in 1746, after the New England and British forces captured it from the French. He took command of Île Royale in 1747 and, under the terms of the treaty of Aix-la-Chapelle, returned the island to the French in July of 1749.

August 4th

The new Halifax School for the Deaf. Shortly after it opened it hosted lectures by Hellen Keller.

1856
The Halifax School for the Deaf first opened on Argyle Street in Halifax. It was the first school for the deaf in Atlantic Canada. William Gray (1806–1881), a deaf immigrant from Scotland, was its first teacher, with two deaf students. Another deaf immigrant from Scotland, George Tait (1828–1904), a self-employed carpenter, was also instrumental in furnishing and raising funds for the school. By 1857, the school had an enrollment of nineteen students, ranging from five years old to twenty-eight. Gray was associated with the school for the next twenty-three years. By 1896, with the support of William Cunard (son of Samuel Cunard), the school opened in new facilities on Gottingen Street, pictured above. It served deaf children from the Atlantic provinces.

August 4th (cont'd)

1891
The *Flying Bluenose* went into operation on the Windsor and Annapolis Railway. It ran from 1891 to 1936, going as far as Yarmouth.

The Flying Bluenose *at Smith's Cove, heading up the Annapolis Valley.*

August 5th

1852
Sir Gaspard Le Marchant (1803–1874) was sworn in as lieutenant governor. He served till February 1858, and later served as governor of Malta from 1859 to 1864. He once wrote, "I am determined to rise to the head of my profession and nothing but death will stop me." He had an illustrious career in the history of the British Army, and founded the British Royal Military College.

August 6th

1890
Yarmouth incorporated as a town. Its first mayor was James J. Lovitt. On August 6, 1892, Yarmouth became the first town to begin an electric streetcar line in the Maritime Provinces (the third in Canada).

August 7th

1966
The Men of the Deeps choir, made up of working and retired coal miners from Cape Breton, was organized as part of the Miner's Folk Society (founded in 1964). The group was an effort to preserve in song some of the rich folklore of the island's coal mining communities. Begun with the vision of Nina Cohen and the leadership of Myles Macdonald as their first executive director, the initiative was also Cape Breton's contribution to Canada's Centennial Year (1967). Since then they travelled across the world. The musical director of the Men of the Deeps was John (Jack) O'Donnell, later a retired professor of music from St. Francis Xavier University in Antigonish. In 1975, O'Donnell published his first collection of coal mining songs entitled *The Men of the Deeps* (preface by Helen Creighton — she had helped in collecting the initial material for the choir). Later in 1992, O'Donnell published a further collection called *And Now the Fields are Green: A Collection of Coal Mining Songs in Canada*. In 2016, O'Donnell was awarded the Dr. Helen Creighton Lifetime Achievement Award at the East Coast Music Awards.

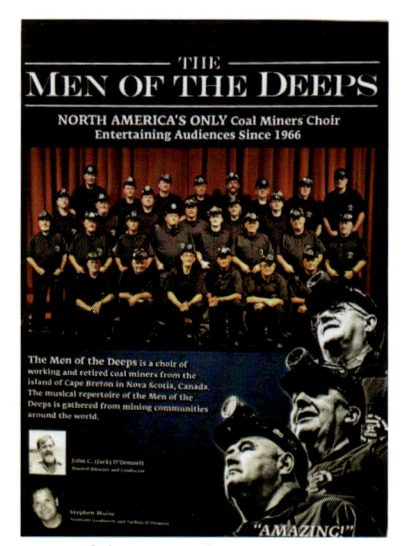

Men of the Deeps choir poster.

August 8th

The Intercolonial Railway Station, Halifax, 1902.

1877
The first official passenger train arrived at the new Intercolonial Railway Station in Halifax. The station was located at the foot of North Street, south of Richmond (Barrington), land that was later below the Angus L. Macdonald Bridge. By 1902 the station was a very busy place.

August 9th

1784
Joseph Frederick Wallet DesBarres (1721–1824) was appointed lieutenant governor of Cape Breton. He served till 1787. He was a noted surveyor and military engineer (present at Ticonderoga in 1757, the fall of Louisbourg in 1758 and at Quebec in 1759). He later resided at Falmouth, not far from Fort Edward, in Castle Frederick. There he worked on surveys that created the *Atlantic Neptune*, an extensive series of naval charts and views that served as standard navigational guides well into the nineteenth century. DesBarres died at the age of 103.

Fort Edward on the Piziquit (Avon) River (Windsor).

August 10th

1909
The Springhill coal mine strike began, lasting till May 1911. A conflict had ensued between the home-grown Provincial Workmen's Association (PWA, formed in 1879), which had represented the miners and which the company was open to negotiate with, and the United Mine Workers of America (UMW), which had won support from the miners but the company refused to recognize. Company ownership of the mine also changed during the strike.

AUGUST 11TH

An Evening View of Halifax, c. 1832, by Henry Samuel Davis.

1787
Captain William Dyott arrived in early July in Halifax as adjutant of the King's Own Regiment of Foot (The Royal Lancasters, known as the 4th). He was also a diarist, and on this day, he had a fishing trip in the harbour, going out around Cornwallis Island (later known as MacNab's Island).

1968
Angus James Walters died (b. in Lunenburg, 1881). He was the first captain of the *Bluenose*, from 1921 to 1938. (Also see *Bluenose*, March 26, 1921 and October 26, 1938.) Walters won five international sailing races and was undefeated for seventeen years. He was one of the first inductees into the Canadian Sports Hall of Fame (inducted in 1955). In 2006, he was recognized as a Person of National Historic Significance in Canada.

AUGUST 12TH

1762
Abbé Pierre Maillard died (b. 1710). A Roman Catholic priest in the Spiritan Order, he arrived at Louisbourg in 1735 as a missionary to the Mi'kmaq. Recognized by the French and British military authorities as an exceptional individual, he was also highly respected by the Mi'kmaq. He assisted in peacemaking and treaties between the British and Mi'kmaq in 1761 and up to the time of his death. He was buried in the Old Burying Ground.

AUGUST 13TH

1953
Family Court Justice Corrine Sparks was born in Loon Lake. She became the first African Nova Scotian to receive an appointment to the judiciary and the first African Canadian female to serve on the bench (1987). Within African Nova Scotian history, Justice Sparks traced her ancestors from the events of the resettlement of the Black Loyalists around 1783.

AUGUST 14ᵀᴴ

1912
The Memorial Tower on the Northwest Arm was dedicated: ". . . Halifax welcomed His Royal Highness Prince Arthur, the Duke of Connaught, the first royal Governor General of Canada, to officially dedicate the Memorial Tower. . . . Sir Sandford Fleming ceremoniously delivered the 1908 title deeds for Sir Sandford Fleming Park to Mayor F.P. Bligh." On April 16, 1908, an Act of Government established the Sir Sandford Fleming Park (called the Dingle), as a gift from Sir Sandford to the City of Halifax. (Also see Fleming, July 22, 1915.)

(TOP) Dingle Tower.
(LEFT) Sandford Fleming.

AUGUST 15ᵀᴴ

1844
After holding their first National Acadian Convention at the Collège Saint-Joseph at Memramcook (NB), the Acadians designated this day as their national day of celebration. This day is also the Roman Catholic Feast of the Assumption of the Blessed Virgin Mary. The Société Nationale l'Assomption (SNA) was created during this convention to organize the annual conventions and be a voice of the Acadian people to various levels of government. At their second National Convention (1884), delegates decided on a flag and an anthem, *"Ave Maris Stella,"* and a motto, *"Strength through unity."* At their third convention, in 1890 at Pointe de L'Église (Church Point), the Collège Sainte-Anne was opened — later known as the Université Sainte-Anne.

The Acadian flag, made official in 1884.

August 15th (cont'd)

(TOP) Ngoon Lee (Chuck's father), Chuck Lee (nine years old, Albert Lee's father) and Lee Wye Ark, Barrington Street Studio, Halifax, 1917.
(LEFT) Halifax Chinese community members posed in front of the Chinese Benevolent Association on Grafton Street in Halifax, on Victory over Japan Day in 1945.

1945

The Chinese community in Halifax gathered at the Chinese Benevolent Association on Grafton Street, Halifax, to celebrate Victory over Japan Day (VJ Day). As photographer Albert Lee pointed out, Chinese immigrants started to arrive in Nova Scotia in the late 1800s. Over 17,000 had been recruited to help build the Canadian Pacific Railway. After its completion, many either returned to China, remained in British Columbia or moved to Eastern Canada. Lee's own father, Chuck, arrived in Halifax from China in 1916 as a nine-year-old boy.

August 16th

1802

A ship arrived in Sydney with 299 Highland immigrants. It was estimated that between 1773 and 1803 at least ten vessels bearing Scottish emigrants landed in Nova Scotia. Cape Breton Island was the last substantial area on the Atlantic Coast of North America to be opened to Scottish emigration. Nova Scotia received some 22,000 Scottish immigrants from 1815 to 1838, the majority from the Highlands and Islands. Peak immigration to Cape Breton ended in the 1830s.

August 17th

1965

Treasure hunters were reported killed at Oak Island, NS. The Associated Press wrote, "A six-year $200,000 hunt for a legendary pirate treasure has ended in death for Robert Restall, his son and two others. The four men died Tuesday on tiny Oak Island, off Nova Scotia's south coast. They were overcome by gas in a shaft 27 feet deep, one of about 200 bored by treasure seekers in the past 170 years. Two treasure hunters who escaped from the shaft thought the men were overcome by 'swamp gas.' Others theorized that a gasoline pump engine over the mouth of the pit had filled the hole with carbon monoxide . . ."

Franklin Delano Roosevelt (third from right, with pipe) on Oak Island in 1909.

August 18th

The SS Royal William, *1834.*

1833
The *Royal William* sailed for England from Pictou, to prove a steamship could make the transatlantic crossing. Considered the fastest ship of its day, it was commissioned by brewer John Molson and a group of investors (including Samuel Cunard from Halifax) and launched from Quebec in 1831.

1930
Government took control of the selling liquor in the province. A plebiscite taken in October 1929 saw 87,647 vote in favour of government control (to 56,082). Prohibition had been enacted in 1921 after a plebiscite in October of 1920.

August 19th

1869
Windsor & Annapolis Railway officially opened between Annapolis and Grand Pré. The Railway proclaimed: "Welcome to the Land of Gabriel and Evangeline." Its corporate successor, the Dominion Atlantic Railway, promoted the "Evangeline Route" for more than eighty years. But it wasn't till the Yarmouth Steamship Company inaugurated its service between Boston and Nova Scotia in the late 1880s that summer visitors started coming.

August 20th

2014
Hugh Alan 'Buddy' MacMaster died in Judique, Nova Scotia (b. 1924). He was a much loved and renowned artist of traditional Cape Breton fiddle music, and considered a true ambassador of Canadian music and a mentor to many. (Also see Natalie MacMaster, June 13, 1972.) He was a recipient of the Order of Canada (2000), the Order of Nova Scotia (2003) and an honorary doctorate from Cape Breton University (2006).

August 21st

1857

A wedding party was hosted in Halifax by Mali Kristia'n Po'l (anglicized to 'Marie-Christiane Paul,' also Christina, Christy Ann, 1804–1886), a Mi'kmaw basketry, beadwork and porcupine quillwork artist and model, with her husband, Thomas Morris (Maurice), for their adopted daughter, Charlotte, to Louis Paul, a young man from Hants. As the mother-in-law, Marie wore "a bright scarlet bodice and richly flounced pink skirt . . . a lady well known and respected," and considered "one of Halifax's most interesting citizens in the 19th century." She was remembered as a talented artist.

2011

A memorial celebration for friends and residents of the Carmelite Hermitage Nova Nada monastery (1972–1998) was held at the fifty-six acre Birchdale property. The monastery had been closed due to clearcut logging that had begun near the property. It was later purchased in 2002 to create a secular, rustic, no-frills getaway retreat setting.

Mary Christianne Paul (Morris) of Chocolate Lake, Halifax, Joseph S. Rogers.

August 22nd

1962

The Halifax Advisory Committee on Human Rights was formed ". . . at the invitation of several residents of Africville, to advise in matters related to an anticipated clearance of the Africville land area for industrial use." — Chairman H.A.J. Wedderburn in a letter to His Worship the Mayor and Aldermen, City of Halifax.

Later the committee would be called the Nova Scotia Humans Rights Federation.

August 23rd

Town and Harbour of Halifax as it Appears from George's Island Looking Up to King's Yard and Basin, Dominic Serres, c.1762.

1766
Michael Francklin (Franklin, 1733–1782) was sworn in as lieutenant governor, serving till 1772. He came to Nova Scotia in 1752 and became a successful colonial merchant and politician. He was captured by a band of Mi'kmaq in 1754, but was released after three months. He also spoke French and was influential among the Acadians, allowing them to return following the expulsion to resettle in NS. He was first elected to the House of Assembly in 1759, and appointed to the Nova Scotia Council in 1762. (Also see, With encouragement... May 13, 1770.)

August 24th

1858
Sir William Fenwick Williams (1800–1883), hero of the Crimean War (1853–1856), returned to Halifax. He was born in Annapolis Royal and became a renowned military leader for the British during the Victorian era, serving in Turkey at Constantinople and in Anatolia. His gallantry was in defence of the town of Kars against the Russians in the Crimean War. Though defeated and imprisoned, he was released at the end of the war in 1856. He also served in the British Parliament and from 1859 to 1864 served as commander in chief, North America. He served as the first Lieutenant Governor of Nova Scotia under Queen Victoria from 1865 to 1867.

August 25th

1910
Actress and dancer Ruby Keeler was born in Dartmouth (d. 1993). When she was a young child, her family moved to New York where she became a dancer and actress, starring in such hits as *42nd Street* (1933) and *No, No, Nanette* (1971).

Ruby Keeler, c. 1935.

400 YEARS IN 365 DAYS

August 26th

1814
The Castine expedition set sail from Halifax under Sir John Coape Sherbrooke (1764–1830), commander of the British forces in the Atlantic area. War with the United States had begun in June 1812, and a long-disputed borderland issue had broken out in the Passamaquoddy Bay area and the Penobscot River where the expedition was headed. They made landfall at Castine. During a successful eight-month occupation, the expedition yielded substantial customs revenues, which financed Dalhousie College and the Garrison Library (later named the Cambridge Military Library). In 1816, Coape was appointed governor general of British North America.

August 27th

1929
Irving Schwartz was born in New Waterford (d. 2010). He became a noted businessman, community leader, philanthropist and humanitarian. After completing his education, he managed his parent's small clothing store and later expanded into other business opportunities. He was involved extensively in many volunteer service organizations. He was awarded Officer of the Order of Canada in 2004 (four years after his sister, Ruth Goldbloom).

Irving Schwartz, July 2007, in the Cape Breton Highlands.

2016
The Last Steps memorial was recognized on the Halifax waterfront to pay tribute to the departure of the first full battalion of Nova Scotia soldiers to fight in the First World War, and the role that Nova Scotia played in the defence of the nation during wartime — a project of the Army Museum Halifax Citadel, designed by artist Nancy Keating.

The Last Steps Memorial, a project of the Army Museum Halifax Citadel, designed by artist Nancy Keating.

August 28th

1781
Annapolis Royal was captured and plundered by American privateers. Prominent citizens, John Ritchie and Thomas Williams were taken hostage, but later released.

August 29th

1911
The Naval Service of Canada was given royal sanction, becoming the Royal Canadian Navy. On May 4, 1910, the *Naval Service Act* had established the Canadian Navy. In addition to a regular force, the *Act* also included a reserve and a naval volunteer force, and a Royal Naval College, located in Halifax. The first Canadian servicemen to die in combat during the First World War were four cadets from this Royal Naval College — all born in Nova Scotia, who served as midshipmen in the Royal Navy.

Captain Martin and naval cadets, Royal Naval College, Halifax, NS, 1912–13.

2012
Ruth Miriam Goldbloom (née Schwartz) died (born 1923). Born in New Waterford, she was educated at Mount Allison and McGill, where she met her husband, Richard Goldbloom. They moved to Halifax in 1967. She became an active community member and fundraiser in many causes, such as health, the post-secondary sector and cultural institutions. Most notably, she co-founded the Pier 21 Society in 1990, with founding President John P. LeBlanc and many other volunteers, raising $16 million to create a new museum at the pier, which opened in 1999. It was designated the National Museum of Immigration in 2009. (Also see, Halifax's Pier 21... January 22, 2009.) She was awarded many honorary degrees, made an Officer of the Order of Canada in April 2000 and awarded the Order of Nova Scotia in 2008 for her dedicated volunteer work in social, religious and heritage organizations in the province.

August 30th

1894
The first meeting of the Executive of Halifax Council of Women occurred at Government House, with Mrs. J.C. Macintosh as president and Anna Leonowens as recording secretary.

August 31st

1843
Our Lady of Sorrows Roman Catholic Church on South Park Street, Halifax, was built in a day. The Holy Cross Cemetery surrounds it on a western-sloping hill.

Holy Cross Cemetery.

SEPTEMBER

September 1st

Delegates to the Charlottetown Conference, 1864, by George P. Roberts.

1864
The Charlottetown Conference was held on Prince Edward Island, with thirty-six men meeting to discuss union amongst the Maritime colonies. But this intention was overwhelmed with discussions about a larger union.

1996
The Puck Starts Here was published by Goose Lane Editions. Author Garth Vaughan provided the critical research and background to the origins of ice hockey in Canada — with the evidence that the early development of the game began in Windsor, Nova Scotia, in 1800 — with King's College students playing an Irish field game called "Hurley-on-Ice." Between 1840 and 1860, the game became known as "Ice Hockey," to describe the game that was starting to be played further afield. From learning the game's early rules, to how the first skates, sticks and pucks were made, along with informative anecdotes about the first Stanley Cup, Vaughan provided a rich history of hockey's beginnings.

September 2nd

1750
The first service was held at St. Paul's Church. Services were conducted by Reverend William Tutty (1715–1754), who served as the first minister from 1750 to 1754. St. Paul's is the oldest surviving Protestant church (Anglican tradition) in Canada and the oldest building in Halifax, designated as a National Historic Site in Canada in 1981. It was built from timbers cut in Boston. St. Paul's was designated as Halifax's first garrison church, and it was mandatory for all military personnel to attend Divine Service.

St. Paul's Church, by William Eager, 1839.

SEPTEMBER 3RD

1783
Colonel Stephen Blucke (1752–1792) with his wife Margaret, and two servants, led an all-black regiment called the Black Pioneers who had fought for the British during the American Revolution to settle in Birchtown, Shelburne County, Nova Scotia. Birchtown was named in honour of Brigadier-General Sam Birch, who issued "certificates of freedom" to the freed blacks who had evacuated New York. Blucke has been referred to as "the true founder of the Afro-Nova Scotian community." In 1788, at his home on the Birchtown Road in Shelburne, Blucke entertained Prince William Henry. The house was designated a Historic Site on July 20, 1996. (Also see A fleet of fifteen ships, January 15, 1792.)

Passport for Cato Ramsay, by order of Brigadier General Birch, April 21, 1783.

SEPTEMBER 4TH

1981
Visual artist Jack L. Gray died in West Palm Beach, Florida. Born in Halifax in 1927 and educated at the Nova Scotia School of Art and Design, he studied at the Montreal Museum of Fine Arts under Arthur Lismer. He spent several seasons at sea with the dory-fishing schooner fleet out of Lunenburg, sketching and taking photographs of marine scenes. After he moved to New York City, he produced a body of oil-on-canvas works depicting marine settings. After further travels, he returned to Nova Scotia in the 1960s. He wintered in West Palm Beach, where he enjoyed the coastal waters of Florida. His ashes were spread near the entrance of Lunenburg Bay. In 2006, Gray's work *Man at Sea* sold at Christie's for $91,200.

Doreymen on the Western Bank, by Jack Gray.

September 5th

Eliza Ritchie (1856–1933).

1933

Eliza Ritchie died (b. 1856). A scholar, author, educator, liberal humanist and feminist, she was the daughter of John W. Ritchie, a Nova Scotia Father of Confederation. She was educated at Dalhousie University and Cornell (Philosophy), and was a cousin to the Canadian diplomat and author, Charles Ritchie. She is considered the first female graduate of a Canadian university to earn a PhD. In 1927, she was the first woman to receive an honorary LLD from Dalhousie. Ritchie was a charter member of the NS Museum of Fine Arts, a forerunner of the Art Gallery of Nova Scotia. She urged the provision of libraries in public schools and the teaching of art to schoolchildren. She led campaigns to reform municipal politics, hold school board elections and achieve women's suffrage. On May 2, 1917, she wrote in the *Halifax Herald* that "It is not for any little group of 'intellectuals' in Halifax and a few other towns that we desire political freedom, we want the great mass of our people, men and women both, [to] be sensible of, and to exercise their responsibility for, the good government of the country."

1755

At their parish church at Grand Pré, a group of Acadian men (418) were officially told by Lieutenant Colonel John Winslow that they and their families were all being deported from the area. On July 28, the Nova Scotia Council had officially announced that the British Crown was removing all Acadians from Nova Scotia. The "first wave" of the deportation orders began on August 10 at Chignecto, after the Battle of Beauséjour. Later orders followed at Grand Pré (location of the largest of the Deportations, totalling 2,700 people — first on October 8, then again in late October), next at Piziquid (Windsor/Falmouth) and lastly at Annapolis Royal on December 8. There were further deportations in November at Memramcook. In 1758, a second wave of deportations occurred at Louisbourg, Petitcodiac River, Restigouche, Saint John, Île St. Jean (PEI) and the Gulf of St. Lawrence. In 1761, a further group were deported from Halifax. Before all these deportations, the Acadian population was estimated at 14,000. Over 11,500 were deported, with 2,500 remaining. Some did go into hiding, escaping to Quebec or hidden among the Mi'kmaq, while others were allowed to stay and repair dykelands that had been damaged by storms.

Deportation-Cross.

September 6th

1985
The Nova Scotia feminist newspaper *Pandora* began publishing from Halifax, "written by women, for women and about women.'" Twenty-nine issues were published.

The Nova Scotia feminist newspaper, Pandora.

1934
Lockeport native, actor and radio announcer Hugh Mills began a children's show on CHNS radio known as *Uncle Mel's*. He read comics to children for fifteen minutes six days a week. The show lasted fifteen years.

September 7th

2006
Dr. Mayann Elizabeth Francis (b. 1946 in Sydney) became the thirty-first lieutenant governor of Nova Scotia. She was the first black person to hold the vice-regal position, and the second woman to serve in this role. The daughter of an Archpriest of the African Orthodox Church, her parents were both born in the Caribbean, relocating to Sydney in the early 1940s from New York City. She grew up in Whitney Pier. Before her appointment as lieutenant governor she was the CEO of the NS Human Rights Commission (1999–2006) and the first woman provincial ombudsman (2000–2003). In 2010, Francis invoked a royal prerogative and granted Canada's first posthumous pardon to Viola Desmond, an African Nova Scotian who, in 1946, insisted on sitting in the whites-only section of a New Glasgow movie theatre. (Also see Viola Desmond, February 7, 1965.)

Mayann E. Francis.

September 8th

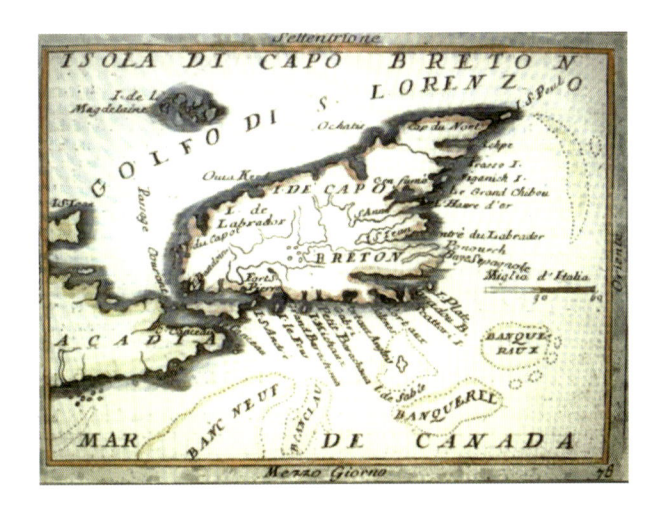

1629
Captain Charles Daniel of the French attacked Sir James Stewart, the fourth Lord Ochiltree of Killeith's settlement on Cape Breton. Known as the Siege of Baleine, Daniel captured the fort and the colonists were taken prisoner. Daniel later built Fort Sainte Anne on the site, and it was named Port Dauphin. After the fall of Louisbourg in 1758 it was called St. Ann's.

One of the earliest known maps to show Cape Breton on its own. Published by Appresso Girolamo Albrizzi, 1697.

September 9th

1843
Thomas McCulloch died in Halifax (b. 1776). He was a prominent Presbyterian minister, educator, author and office holder. Born in 1776 in Scotland, he settled in Pictou in 1803. He became the principal of Pictou Academy and, in 1838, the first president of Dalhousie University. He was author of the satirical "Letters of Mephibosheth Stepsure."

Thomas McCulloch (1776–1843), the first president of Dalhousie University. AST, by D. MacGee.

The Fire in Granville Street, by H.H. Laird, 1859.

1859
Over two blocks of Granville Street in Halifax (including sixty buildings) were destroyed by fire.

September 10th

1944
Winston Churchill (1874–1965) arrived in Halifax en route to Quebec to attend the Quebec Conference (held from September 12 to 16) between the British and American governments, hosted by Canada. A year earlier, Churchill had come through Halifax in secret for the first Quebec Conference. For security reasons, Halifax at the time was designated the "East Coast Port."

1954
Henry D. Hicks (1915–1990) was elected leader of the NS Liberal Party. Hicks became an MLA in 1945, and was premier from 1954 to 1956, when he lost to Robert Stanfield's Progressive Conservatives. He resigned as Leader of the Opposition in 1960 and joined Dalhousie University. He was president of Dalhousie from 1963 till 1980.

1939
Canada declared war on Germany.

Editorial cartoonist Bob Chambers's visual take on Churchill's "secret" visit to Halifax in 1943.

September 11th

Nova Scotia Government House, 1819. Etching by J.E. Woolford.

1800
The cornerstone of Nova Scotia Government House was laid by Governor John Wentworth. It is the oldest official government residence in Canada. In 1819, while he served as an aide to the Lieutenant Governor Lord Dalhousie, J.E. Woolford created a sketch of the residence.

1749
On this day, Colonel Cornwallis wrote to the Board of Trade concerning the status of the fort at the top of Citadel Hill. This was the first of four generations of forts built on the hill. The last one started in 1828 and took thirty years to complete. The two-year period (1869–71) when the 78th Highlanders were garrisoned in Halifax became the focal point of Parks Canada and the Halifax Citadel's Regimental Association's presentation of the fort's history.

Halifax Citadel National Historic Site of Canada.

400 YEARS IN 365 DAYS

September 12th

2014

African Nova Scotian poet and educator Maxine Tynes died (b. 1949). She was an acclaimed poet (winner of the Milton Acorn People's Poetry Award) and dedicated high school teacher. In 1986, she also became the first African Canadian woman to sit on Dalhousie's Board of Governors, serving until 1994. Tynes is quoted as saying, "My poems are great shouts of the joy that I feel and share; the deep passion that rocks and caresses and embraces me and all that is part of my world and my life. The laments for lost heritage are there; but, then, so are the feelings of having found a centre and a self-acceptance and an identity in this Black and woman's skin that I so joyfully wear . . . I wear it joyfully. I wear it big. I wear it womanly. And I wear it Black. Black. Black. As night, deep and soft and endless with no moon. Just black and perfect splendour in life and in being a woman in this world."

September 13th

1984

Pope John Paul II visited Halifax and spoke to an estimated crowd of 75,000 on the North Commons.

Pope John Paul II on the Halifax Common, 1984.

September 14th

1767

Captain William Owen (1737–1778) began his exploratory tour of Nova Scotia, journeying from Halifax to Minas Basin via Dartmouth Lakes and the Shubenacadie River. Owen had been commissioned by Nova Scotia Governor Lord William Campbell (1730–1778), whom Owen had served in India and Nova Scotia.

1853

The first sod of the European and North American Railway (E&NA) was turned by Lady Anna Maria Head, the wife of New Brunswick Lieutenant Governor Edmund Head (he later served as governor general of Canada from 1854 to 1861). The railway, was conceived at a railway conference in Portland, Maine in 1850 by railroad entrepreneur John A. Poor, intended to link Portland (the eastern terminus of the US rail network) with an ice free Atlantic port in Nova Scotia at Halifax. By 1860, the E&NA line had only made it to Moncton.

September 15th

The Hector at Heritage Quay on Pictou's historic waterfront.

1773
The *Hector* arrived at Pictou. After a voyage of eleven weeks, the ship landed at Brown's Point with 189 settlers (having lost eighteen on the voyage to dysentery and smallpox). The settlers originated from Lochbroom — Northern Scottish Highlanders who spoke mainly Gaelic. The provisions they were promised didn't materialize and they had to quickly build shelter before winter set in.

September 16th

A convoy of merchant ships in the Bedford Basin, April 1, 1942.

1939
The maiden Second World War convoy of eighteen merchant vessels sailed from Halifax for Britain. Over 377 convoys sailed from September 16, 1939 to May 23, 1945, during the Battle of the Atlantic — representing a total of 25,343 merchant ships. The battle claimed more than 70,000 Allied seamen, merchant mariners and airmen, including 2,024 Royal Canadian Navy personnel and 1,629 Merchant Navy seafarers. Each year on the first Sunday of May, the naval community commemorates those lost at sea during the Second World War. (Also see HMCS *St. Croix*, September. 20, 1943, and Admiralty House, January. 1, 1819.)

September 17th

1999
The Supreme Court of Canada affirmed in the Donald Marshall case a 5–2 decision regarding treaty rights to hunt, fish and gather in pursuit of a moderate livelihood, stemming from the treaties of 1760–1761 that were signed by the Mi'kmaq, Malisset, Passamaquoddy and the British Crown. The Supreme Court did not define how these rights were to be implemented, but instead encouraged the parties to negotiate a resolution in a fair and equitable manner. Shortly after, the Nova Scotia Office of Aboriginal Affairs was established to represent the province through the terms of the Mi'kmaq–Nova Scotia–Canada Framework Agreement, which was signed in February 2007 to address issues related to Mi'kmaq treaty and Aboriginal rights and title in Nova Scotia. Donald Marshall, Jr. died on August 6, 2009 (b. 1953).

September 18th

2012
Award-winning Canadian Celtic folk musician Mary Jane Lamond and fiddler Wendy MacIsaac released their album *Seinn*. It was named one of the top ten folk and Americana albums of 2012 by the National Public Radio in the United States.

Seinn, released in 2012.

September 19th

1839
Albion Mines Railroad, Nova Scotia's first steam railway, opened between Stellarton and Pictou Harbour, hauling coal to the pier. There were three locomotives assigned to the job, called Samson, Hercules and John Buddle. This marked the province's entry into the industrial revolution. The railroad and mines were operated by a London-based firm, the General Mining Association, "which held an exclusive lease of nearly all the mineral rights in Nova Scotia" from 1828 to 1858. Samson became the oldest surviving original Canadian locomotive — the first to burn coal and run on all-steel rails.

September 20th

1943
The Canadian naval destroyer HMCS *St. Croix*, commanded by Lieutenant Commander A.H. Dobson (age forty-two), was torpedoed by the German submarine, U-305, while she was protecting convoys, which were heavily "beset by a wolfpack" south of Iceland as they sailed toward Nova Scotia. The *St. Croix* sank in six minutes, with the loss of 146 lives. (A list of the men lost can be found at uboat.net.) Most were under thirty. Allied losses in the convoy were three escorts and six ships sunk, and one escort and one ship damaged. Three U-boats were destroyed and three damaged and forced to return to their base. (Also see Convoys, September 16, 1939.)

September 21st

1932
A bust of Sir Walter Scott (1771–1832) was unveiled by the North British Society at the entrance to the Public Gardens on the hundredth anniversary of Scott's death. He was a noted Scottish historical novelist, playwright and poet with many contemporary readers in Europe, Australia and North America. The bust was created by Sir Francis Leggatt Chantrey, who was at the time a leading English sculptor.

Bust of Sir Walter Scott.

2014
The inaugural Lunenburg Doc Film Festival (September 21–23) began. In 2017, the fourth annual festival was expanded to four days of documentary film screenings, celebrations, free youth and senior programs, free community and educational events and an industry symposium for filmmakers.

September 22nd

(TOP) Halifax Dartmouth Bridge, by LeRoy Zwicker.
(LEFT) Peggy's Cove, by Marguerite Zwicker.

1993
Visual artist Marguerite Zwicker died in Halifax. She was born in Yarmouth in 1904 and studied at the Nova Scotia College of Art. She later taught painting at Acadia University, and married fellow artist Leroy Zwicker (1906–1987). In 1957 they took over Zwicker's Gallery, the oldest gallery in Halifax (founded in 1886). Until the establishment of the Art Gallery of Nova Scotia and the university art galleries in the 1970s, their gallery was the only venue in Halifax where art was regularly shown to the public.

1901
Charles Huggins was born in Halifax (d. 1997). He was a Nobel Prize winner in medicine, and graduate of Acadia University (1920). The award was ". . . for discovering in 1941 that hormones could be used to control the spread of some cancers." Huggins was also chancellor of Acadia from 1972 to 1979.

September 23rd

1835
The first installment of Thomas Chandler Haliburton's *The Clockmaker* was published in the *Novascotian* by Joseph Howe under the title *Recollections of Nova Scotia*. Haliburton presented a total of twenty-two sketches, which were published in 1836 as a first series collection titled *The Clockmaker, or, the Sayings and Doings of Samuel Slick of Slicksville*. It was hugely popular, not only in Nova Scotia but also in Britain and the United States. A second series was published in London in 1838 and a third series in 1840. Haliburton published numerous further works. In 1858, he was the first colonial to receive an honorary doctorate for services to literature from Oxford University. He died in England, eight weeks after Nova Scotia joined Confederation.

Thomas Chandler Haliburton.

SEPTEMBER 24TH

1974
The weekly tabloid the *Bedford-Sackville News* began publishing. It expanded to six days a week in 1979. By 1981 it was renamed the *Daily News*, gaining a reputation for hard-hitting provincial news stories. The paper was bought out in 1985 and the original publishers began *Frank* magazine in 1987, focused on gossip and the private lives of the well-heeled and famous in the Maritime Provinces. In March 2001, they began the online news service AllNovaScotia.com.

SEPTEMBER 25TH

1726
Acadian deputies in the district around Annapolis Royal were summoned before Lieutenant Governor Lawrence Armstrong to sign an unqualified oath of allegiance. They insisted on freedom of religion and exemption from bearing arms. No agreement was reached. A year later, the inhabitants were encouraged by a written confirmation of a military exemption, but this was not ratified further. The Acadians mistakenly believed that they were entitled to neutrality in war time. This issue arose once again with the arrival of Governor Edward Cornwallis.

SEPTEMBER 26TH

1832
After travelling in the United States, Upper and Lower Canada and New Brunswick, British Lieutenant E.T. Coke arrived in Nova Scotia in September. He made his way from Saint John, NB, to Digby, sailing up to Annapolis Royal and then going by coach up to Bridgetown and on to Kentville, where he stayed the night. He left the next morning for Windsor, where he stayed overnight, before leaving on his last leg of the journey to Halifax.

1959
A.R. Mosher, former president of the Canadian Labour Congress and a native of Halifax, died.

SEPTEMBER 27TH

1948
The Seahorse Tavern opened on Argyle Street in Halifax (for men only). Taverns had been closed in 1916 during the First World War. The Seahorse was the first to be allowed to open in Halifax. It moved to Gottingen Street in 2014.

The Seahorse Tavern, 1947.

September 28th

2012

The Pictou Landing Native Women's Association / Group (PLNWG) announced a training initiative to support their multi-year, community, based, participatory Health Survey Training Plan — *Identifying, Documenting, Mapping, and Mobilizing Environment and Health Knowledge in Pictou Landing: An Environmental Health Survey.* Out of concern for their children, families, and community, the PLNWG mobilized around the issue of Boat Harbour in 2010 to address the question, "Is Boat Harbour making us sick?" The Pictou Landing First Nations borders on Boat Harbour. From 1965, the harbour had been the source for dumping effluent waste from the Abercrombie Point Pulp and Paper Mill. In 2016, the PLNWG released their final report: *Our Ancestors Are in Our Land, Water, and Air — A Two-Eyed Seeing Approach to Researching Environmental Health Concerns with Pictou Landing First Nation.*

September 29th

1965

Ross Douglas Hamilton died (b. 1889). Known as 'Marjorie' in the Dumbells, he was a talented female impersonator from Pugwash, Nova Scotia. He had enlisted as a private with the Canadian Army during the First World War and served as an ambulance driver in France before being selected by Captain Merton Plunkett to join the Dumbells Canadian Army Third Division Concert Party as a soldier-entertainer. The Dumbells gained popularity across Canada and internationally after the war, touring North America as a vaudeville act until 1932. Hamilton rejoined the Army Medical Corps in the Second World War. In August 1941, Hamilton was quietly discharged from the army "for reasons other than medical," allegedly for homosexual behaviour with some of the recruits. After the war, he continued as a professional entertainer, eventually retiring to Nova Scotia.

Ross Douglas Hamilton.

September 30th

1749

Soon after a written warning to Cornwallis, forty Mi'kmaq and Acadian warriors led by Beausoleil Broussard surprised a wood-cutting crew at Major Gilman's sawmill in Dartmouth. Two men were scalped, and three were decapitated; one escaped to sound the alarm. This was the first of numerous Mi'kmaq attacks which kept the settlers ill at ease and within the palisades of Halifax. (Also see, During the first...March 26, 1751.)

Memorial plaque to the raid on Dartmouth, 1749.

October

October 1st

2000
A historic plaque ceremony commemorating the Mi'kmaq cultural landscape took place at Kejimkujik National Park in recognition of the Mi'kmaq presence there since time immemorial. The park has the largest concentration of Mi'kmaq petroglyphs in eastern North America. By 2013, Parks Canada had to prohibit visiting the petroglyphs without permission in order to protect this important cultural resource.

European vessel with stick figures, n.d., one of Kejimkujik's petroglyph rock carvings.

1867
Susannah Woodhouse (Culverwell) Oland (1818–1885) and her husband, John James Dunn Oland (1819–1870), began their brewery in Dartmouth at Turtle Grove, later to be named The Army and Navy Brewery — a name that came from their most appreciative customers. After John Oland's untimely death in 1870, Susannah, with her three sons and the support of investors, changed the name to S. Oland, Sons and Co, continuing to run the brewery from their Turtle Grove site. The Dartmouth-based brewery was later destroyed in the Halifax Explosion, killing Susannah's son Conrad and six other employees. It was later rebuilt, and the family branched out to New Brunswick.

Turtle Grove Brewery Workers, 1890s.

October 2nd

A Modern Conception of the Maid Evangeline, by Amos Lawson Hardy, c. 1917.

1935
Nova Scotia photographer Amos Lawson Hardy died in Kentville (b. 1860). As noted in the *Morning Herald* on October 4, his photographic works were "sold in all parts of the world" and were a catalyst in advertising and promoting Nova Scotia, especially the Annapolis Valley Land of Evangeline, as a tourist destination.

October 3rd

1914
The first Canadian Contingent left for England in the largest convoy to cross the Atlantic in the First World War. Over the course of the war, more than 650,000 Canadians made that crossing. More than 66,000 did not return. (Also see The Last Steps, August 27, 2016.)

October 4th

The Industrial Exhibition Building at Halifax, Nova Scotia, Robert Wilkie, George DuBois, 1854.

1854
The Great Agricultural and Industrial Exhibition arrived in Halifax for the first time. Inspired by the Great Exhibition at the Crystal Palace in London, the exhibition took over Province House grounds for a week in October.

October 5th

1946
Eddie Carvery was born in Africville. He undertook one of the longest civil rights protests in Canadian history. Beginning in the 1970s, he protested the forced removal of the Africville community in the North End of Halifax in the 1960s. (Also see Africville apology, February 24, 2010.) Carvery's struggle is chronicled in *The Hermit of Africville: The Life of Eddie Carvery* by Jon Tattrie.

1987
Custio Clayton was born in Dartmouth. He took up amateur boxing, winning his first bout at the age of eleven. After finishing high school, he qualified for the 2012 Summer Olympics and became the first Canadian to win a boxing bout in eight years at the Olympics. As of 2016, he was a nine-time Canadian amateur boxing champion.

October 6th

2016
Dalhousie University permanently raised the Mi'kmaq Santé Mawiómi flag, sometimes referred to as the Grand Council flag, as a gesture that the university recognizes that it is located on traditional territory of the Mi'kmaq people. There are differences of opinion on whether the flag should be flown vertically or horizontally. The meaning in the design of the flag:
- *Wapék* (White) — Denotes the purity of Creation
- *Mekwék Klujjewey* (Red Cross) — Represents mankind and infinity (four directions)
- *Nákúset* (Sun) — Forces of the day
- *Tepkunaset* (Moon) — Forces of the night

The Mi'kmaq flag.

October 7th

1763
Île Royale (Cape Breton) was ceded to the British under the terms of the Treaty of Paris and came under the colonial governance of mainland Nova Scotia. The following year, the Acadians who had been expelled were permitted to return. By 1783 and 1784, waves of Loyalist settlers began to arrive (more than 30,000). In 1784, Nova Scotia was divided into three separate colonies: Cape Breton Island, New Brunswick and mainland Nova Scotia. In 1820, the colony of Cape Breton was re-annexed back to mainland Nova Scotia. Cape Breton received a large influx of Highland Scots in the first half of the nineteenth century, with estimates of close to 50,000, as the result of the Highland Clearances.

October 8th

Ron James.

2004
Glace Bay–born comedian Ron James (b. 1958) won in the category for Best Live Comedy Stand-up for *The Road Between My Ears* at the first annual Canadian Comedy Awards in Toronto. He appeared in dozens of commercials, television roles and films.

1885
The first four-masted schooner in Canada, *J.M. Blackie*, launched at Great Village in Colchester County.

October 9th

1882
Oscar Wilde visited Halifax and gave two readings at the Academy of Music. The Academy was located where the Maritime Centre now stands on Barrington Street in Halifax. "Over 1500 Haligonians attended his lecture *The Decorative Arts* and 400 attended a lecture later the next evening on *The House Beautiful*." Three years later, on February 14, 1895, Wilde opened his new play *The Importance of Being Earnest* in London. (Also see Academy, January 9, 1877.)

1997
The Celtic Colours International Festival began, running till October 18. Two Cape Bretoners, Joella Foulds and Max MacDonald, used the hallmarks of Cape Breton — its music and scenery — as the basis for an annual festival, running for nine days. In 2017, the festival ran from October 6 to 14.

Oscar Wilde.

October 10th

2005
Renowned rug hooking artist Elizabeth LeFort died in Chéticamp (b. 1914). She learned to rug hook from her mother at a young age. Particularly skilled at replicating photographs, LeFort created highly detailed portraits, some of which were held in the Vatican Fine Arts Gallery, the White House and Buckingham Palace. The Elizabeth Lefort Gallery displaying her work was opened on August 15, 1983.

Elizabeth LeFort.

October 11th

1942
The RCMP schooner *St. Roch* slipped into Halifax Harbour, ending the first successful west-to-east navigation of the Northwest Passage. The nine-member crew, under the command of Sergeant (later Superintendant) Henry Larsen, left Vancouver in 1940, spending two winters frozen in ice. After a refit in Dartmouth, the ship made its east-to-west transit of the passage in eighty-six days.

The RCMP schooner St. Roch *took on water as it made its way through the Northwest Passage. Photo by Major James Skitt Matthews (1878–1970).*

October 12th

1917
Sir Robert L. Borden formed government in Ottawa (Unionist).

October 13th

1967
Black Friday in Cape Breton — Hawker Siddeley announced the closing of the Sydney steel plant by April 30, 1968. The plant had been purchased from DOSCO in August 1957 and employed 5,700 workers. But declining markets, and lack of further capital investment for refurbishing, led to a reduction in the workforce to 3,200 by 1967. And though there was hope for a recommended expansion of the plant, the company ultimately changed its mind and announced its closure. By November 22, with an Act of the Legislature, the NS government created Sydney Steel Corporation (SYSCO) to operate the plant, which closed in 2001. The plant left a hazardous waste site, known as the Sydney Tar Ponds — which caused one of the most complex environmental cleanup operations ever undertaken in Canada, costing over $400 million.

October 14th

1921
The first issue of the *Maritime Labour Herald* was published, announcing itself as "a paper devoted to the interests of labor." "We are a working class paper in working class dress and right on the job fighting the battle of the working class." Organized by J.B. McLachlan and B.N. Brodie, it was guided by the editorship of William Ulrich Cotton. The paper's circulation reached over 6,000 and continued for five years. (Also see McLachlan, November. 3, 1937.)

1942
While carrying 237 passengers and a crew of forty-five between Sydney and Port-Aux-Basques, the ferry SS *Caribou* was sunk by a German U-Boat, with 136 lives lost.

October 15th

2004
Shirley Burnham Elliott died in Kentville (born 1916). She was a librarian and writer on Nova Scotian history (author of the *Nova Scotia Book of Days*, 1979), a community volunteer and mentor. She was Nova Scotia's legislative librarian from 1954 to 1982, was awarded honorary degrees by Acadia and Dalhousie Universities and was a recipient of the Order of Nova Scotia (2003).

1971
Michelin Tire opened its plant in Bridgewater. Construction on this plant, and one at Granton in Pictou County, had begun in 1970. A third plant in Waterville, King's County, would be announced in 1979. The initial investment was valued at over $100 million, with Michelin providing $35 million, and Nova Scotia Industrial Estates providing $50 million, plus various provincial and federal government grants. The federal government also waived duties for three years related to tire lines not made in Canada. Nearly 3,600 workers were employed at the first two plants.

Shirley Burnham Elliott.

October 16th

2016
African Nova Scotia leader, politician and activist Dr. Lynn Jones, in cooperation with Saint Mary's University, announced the addition of the Lynn Jones African-Canadian & Diaspora Heritage Collection to the University Archives. The collection documented the lives of Lynn, her family and over fifty years of African, African diasporic and African Nova Scotian heritage and history. (Also see Burnley 'Rocky' Jones, July 29, 2013.)

October 17th

1831
The Halifax Mechanics' Library Association was established. Their first president was John S. Thompson. By December a public meeting was held and the Mechanics' Institute was also born, with Dr. William Grigor as its President. Joseph Howe became Vice-President and delivered the opening address on January 11, 1832.

October 18th

1814
The British transport ship *Sovereign* was wrecked off Saint Paul Island, killing 202 British troops, with thirty-seven survivors.

1783
More Loyalist families arrived in Digby. Over a thousand had arrived in May. Digby was named after Rear Admiral Robert Digby (1732–1815), who had brought Loyalists to the area.

October 19th

1901
A cornerstone for the South African War Memorial at Province House was laid by the Duke of York (who became King George V). Earlier, a grand parade had taken place along Granville Street to mark his visit.

A parade along Granville Street marked the visit of HRH the Duke of York (the future King George V). Looking north toward Halifax Harbour and Dartmouth (1901).

October 20th

1803
The Halifax Town Clock, built on the east side of Citadel Hill under the direction of Prince Edward, Duke of Kent, began keeping time for the garrison and town residents. It is said that the prince, then commander in chief of all military forces in British North America, wished to resolve the tardiness of the local garrison. (Also see Prince Edward, June 28, 1794.)

The Old Town Garrison Clock, Halifax, 1895.

October 21st

The armoured cruiser HMCS Niobe, 1910.

1910
The armoured cruiser HMCS *Niobe*, the Canadian Navy's first ship, arrived in Halifax. Already considered obsolescent, she was initially manned by Royal Naval personnel, on loan to the new service.

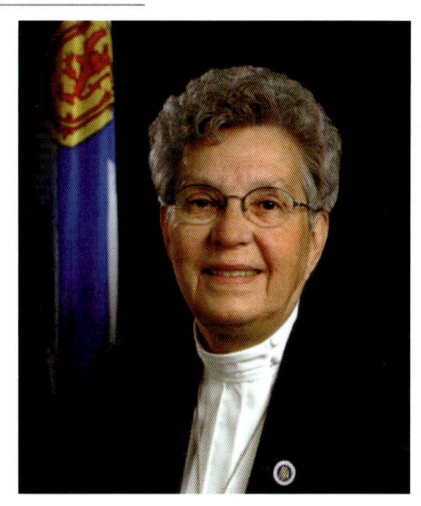

Dorothy Moore.

2003
Mi'kmaw educator Sister Dorothy Moore, received the Order of Nova Scotia (ONS). Born in the Mi'kmaq community of Membertou in 1933, she became a member of the Congregation of Sisters of St. Martha of Antigonish in 1956.

October 22nd

1958
Blanche Margaret Meagher (b. Halifax in 1911) was appointed ambassador to Israel (1958–1961) — Canada's first woman ambassador. From 1969 to 1973 she was ambassador to Sweden, and served in Mexico and England. She was made an Officer of the Order of Canada in 1974.

October 23rd

The Lord Nelson Hotel, Halifax, 1941.

1928
The Lord Nelson Hotel opened in Halifax, on the corner of Spring Garden Road and South Park Street on what was known as the old Dwyer property. It was seven storeys with 200 rooms — named after England's greatest naval hero: Horatio Nelson.

400 YEARS IN 365 DAYS

October 23rd (cont'd)

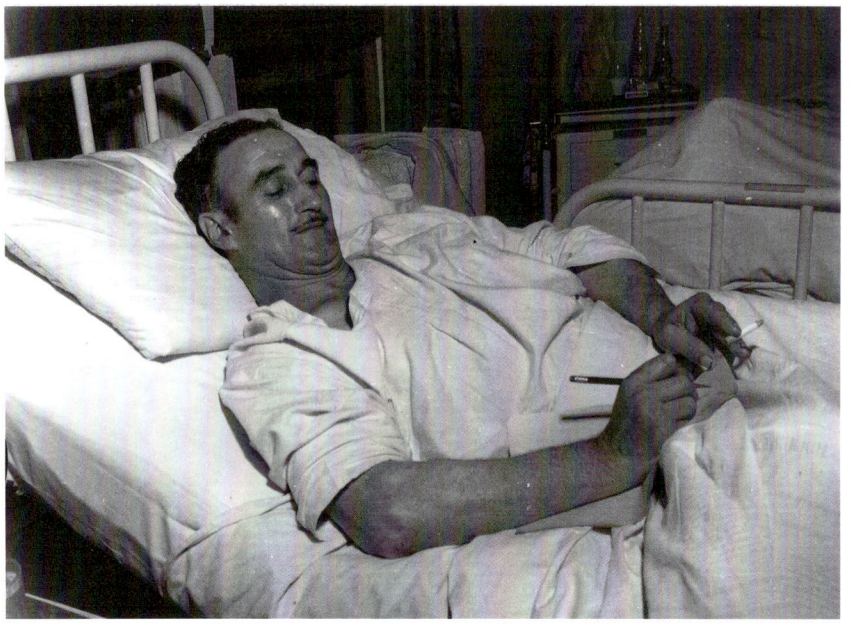

1958
A seismic jolt, known in miner terms as a "bump," occurred in the No. 2 colliery mine at Springhill. There were 174 men working 1,200 metres underground at the time. Seventy-five were killed. Nineteen men who had been trapped were found alive a week later (twelve were found on October 29 and seven on November 1). Forty-six-year-old African Canadian Maurice Ruddick was one of the seven last miners to be found alive. He had a broken leg, but helped his companions keep their spirits up by singing and leading them in song. Ruddick died in 1988.

Maurice Ruddick after the Springhill Mine disaster, 1958.

October 24th

1816
George Ramsay, ninth Earl of Dalhousie (1770–1838), was sworn in as lieutenant governor, serving from 1816 to 1820. He later became the governor general of Canada, and served from 1820 to 1828. He founded Dalhousie College in 1818 at the north end of the Grand Parade (moved in 1886 to a five-acre site on the South Common). He also provided funds for the maintenance of the Garrison Library (renamed the Cambridge Military Library, the oldest military library in Canada), located at Royal Artillery Park in Halifax. While in Nova Scotia, Dalhousie travelled the province and kept extensive diaries. (Also see Royal Artillery Park, October 29, 1934.)

The Right Honourable George Ramsay, Ninth Earl of Dalhousie, by John Elliott Woolford, c. 1840.

October 25th

1951
Louis Armstrong performed at the Queen Elizabeth Auditorium. Tickets were $2.20 (including tax). Besides Armstrong playing trumpet and doing vocals, Jack Teagarden played trombone and vocals, Cozy Cole played drums and Earl 'Fatha' Hines played piano.

Louis Armstrong.

1944
Lieutenant Edward Francis Arab (b. 1915), died at age twenty-nine on the frontlines in the Battle of the Scheldt (Holland). He was one of the youngest graduates of Dalhousie Law School (1937) and was the first president of the Canadian Lebanon Society (1938). He was the son of Louis A. Arab and Sadie Assiff. His paternal grandfather, Abraham, was among the first villagers from Diman (Lebanon) to settle in Nova Scotia. Over 6,367 Canadian soldiers either lost their lives, were wounded or became missing during the Battle of the Scheldt. Edward Francis Arab was laid to rest in the Bergen-op-Zoom Canadian War Cemetery in southwest Holland.

Edward Francis Arab.

October 26th

1938
The *Bluenose* schooner won its last International Fisherman's Cup Race by less than three minutes, winning three races out of five against the *Gertrude L. Thebaud* off Gloucester, Massachusetts.

Bluenose romping across the finish line to win the last race in the International Fishermen's Trophy Series and snatch the championship from the Gertrude L. Thebaud.

400 YEARS IN 365 DAYS

October 27th

Daniel Christmas.

2016
Daniel Christmas (b. 1956), Mi'kmaw leader and lifelong resident of the Membertou First Nation, was named as a "non-partisan" senator, the first Mi'kmaw representative to the Canadian Senate, by Prime Minister Justin Trudeau. Christmas was previously the director of advisory services for the Union of Nova Scotia Indians.

A four-masted barque under repair at Summerville, NS, 1909.

1874
The schooner *W.D. Lawrence* was launched at Maitland — the largest wooden-hulled ship ever built in the Maritimes, at 2,459 tons and a keel length of 244 feet 9 inches. She was named after her builder and owner, William D. Lawrence. The ship cost $107,452 to build. Lawrence sailed it with his family and crew for almost three years and authored an account of their travels in 1880. The ship was sold to a group of Norwegians in 1883.

October 28th

1851
Norman McLeod Sailed from St. Ann's, Nova Scotia to New Zealand.

October 29th

1934
A tablet was unveiled at the Royal Artillery Park in Halifax by Lieutenant Governor Walter H. Covert recognizing the historic importance of the Cambridge Military Library, which had housed the Garrison Library collection since 1817. In 1902, the library was named after Prince George, Duke of Cambridge. (Also see George Ramsay, ninth Earl of Dalhousie, October 24, 1816.)

The Cambridge Military Library.

October 30th

1915
Sir Charles Tupper died at Bexley Heath, Kent, England. A former premier of Nova Scotia, he led the province into Confederation. He was also the last remaining Father of Confederation. (Also see Sir Charles Tupper, July 2, 1821.)

October 31st

1930
The Capitol Theatre opened in Halifax, at the corner of Barrington and Spring Garden Road (later the location of the Maritime Centre). Before the Capitol Theatre, this location was home to the Academy of Music, renamed the Majestic in 1918. It had opened in 1877, and was home to countless musical and theatre productions for over fifty years. It was demolished in 1929. The Capitol was demolished in 1974.

(TOP) The Capitol Theatre opened in Halifax, December 31, 1930.
(BOTTOM) The Capitol Theatre in the year it was torn down, 1974.

NOVEMBER

November 1st

2001
The St. John's Anglican Church in Lunenburg was destroyed by fire. The historic church (completed in 1763) was rebuilt from donations from across the country and around the world. It was reopened on June 12, 2005. The church had been designated a National Historic Site in October, 1998. Canada's oldest Presbyterian (St. Andrew's, 1754) and Lutheran (Zion's, 1772) churches were also in Lunenburg.

(LEFT) The rebuilt St. John's Anglican Church, 2012.
(BELOW) The St. John's Anglican Church after the fire, November 2, 2001.

1956
An explosion occurred at Springhill's No. 4 colliery, 1,900 metres down. Thirty-nine miners were killed. Eighty-eight miners were trapped, but later rescued. This was one of the first disasters with on-site radio broadcast reporting.

1788
King's College opened in Windsor.

1966
The Men of the Deeps choir of Cape Breton performed their first three concerts from November 1 to 3 at the Savoy (Glace Bay), the Vogue (Sydney) and Paramount (New Waterford) theatres. Over 3,000 people attended.

November 2nd

1836
Simon d'Entremont (Argyle) and Frederick Armand Robicheau (Annapolis) became the first French Acadians in North America to be elected to the Nova Scotia General Assembly (the fifteenth Assembly, 1836–1840). Before taking his seat in the House of Assembly, d'Entremont was asked to swear an oath to the British crown. He replied, "You can take back your document . . . I would rather swallow a dogfish, tail first, than swear that." He knew that he was right to refuse to take the oath, as the British Parliament had abolished it eight years earlier. He married twice, with nine children from each marriage, and left over 136 descendants.

Simon d'Entremont.

2015
Anne Fulton died at age sixty-four. A self-employed counsellor, editor and writer, she was considered a "founding mother" of Halifax's gay and lesbian activist community. She was an original member of the Gay Alliance for Equality (1973), and a founder in organizing the Atlantic Provinces Political Lesbians for Equality.

Anne Fulton.

November 3rd

1937
James B. McLachlan died in Glace Bay (b. 1869). A coalminer, union leader, labour leader, farmer and journalist, he arrived in Canada in 1902 to work at the Princess Colliery in Sydney Mines. He became a local leader in the Provincial Workmen's Association (est. in 1879). He wrote in the *Halifax Herald* in January 1908, on the 149th anniversary of Robert Burns's death, "The greatest political question of this century is how to distribute the enormous wealth that the ingenuity of the last century enables the world now to produce." Later he was the leader of the largest union in the province — District 26 of the United Mine Workers. (Also see the first issue, October 14, 1921.)

James B. McLachlan.

November 4th

1967
G.I. Smith was chosen as leader of the Progressive Conservative Party. He was noted for having recruited Robert Stanfield to help rebuild the party. Smith served as an MLA from 1949 to 1974 (was Premier from 1967 to 1970), and later a senator from 1975 to 1982.

November 5th

1789
Nova Scotia's first agricultural society was formed in Horton, Kings County. It was originally known as the Colonial Societias — its founders were mainly New England Planters who immigrated to Nova Scotia after the expulsion of the Acadians. In 1805 the Society changed its name to the Kings County Central Agricultural Society.

November 6th

The poorhouse, or Poors Asylum, after a fire of 1882.

1882
A serious fire took place at the Provincial Poor Asylum. Thirty-one people died (out of 343 residents), more lives lost than in any other fire in the city's history. "The Poor Asylum or Poor House was the primary institution for the care of the elderly, mentally ill and poor. Originally situated on Spring Garden Road at the present site of the Halifax Memorial Library, it was relocated to the South Common in 1866" (Halifax and Its People 1749–1999, *Nova Scotia Archives, 1999*).

November 7th

Princess Elizabeth with Prince Philip (1951).

1951
Princess Elizabeth (who became Queen Elizabeth II) visited Nova Scotia with Prince Philip.

November 8th

2016
Dr. Frances Wagner died in Falmouth, NS (b. Hamilton, Ontario, 1917). A feminist scientific pioneer, she was educated at the University of Toronto and Stanford University. In 1950, at the age of twenty-three, she began undertaking field research with the Geological Survey of Canada in the James Bay region. Her specialty was micropaleontology, in which she became a distinguished expert, providing insight into biogeological prehistory, and leading the way for other women in non-traditional fields. She arrived in Halifax in 1967 to work with the Bedford Institute of Oceanography (BIO).

Dr. Frances Wagner, centre, received a service certificate marking twenty-five years with the Geological Survey of Canada, in Dartmouth, NS, in 1975. To her left and right, respectively, were colleagues Dr. Dale Buckley and Dr. Bosko Loncarevic.

November 9th

1990
Novelist and essayist John Hugh MacLennan died in Montreal (b. 1907 in Glace Bay). His family moved to Halifax when he was seven. He was educated at the Halifax Academy and Dalhousie University, attended Oxford on a Rhodes Scholarship, and later Princeton. He worked as a professor of English at McGill, but by 1945 he began writing full-time, winning five Governor General's Awards. Some of his noted novels include *Barometer Rising* (1941), set during the Halifax Explosion of 1917; *Two Solitudes* (1945); *Each Man's Son* (1951); and *The Watch That Ends the Night* (1957), from which this except comes: "But that night as I drove back from Montreal, I at least discovered this: that there is no simple explanation for anything important any of us do, and that the human tragedy, or the human irony, consists in the necessity of living with the consequences of actions performed under the pressure of compulsions so obscure we do not and cannot understand them."

Hugh MacLennan.

November 10th

1900
The paddle steamer *City of Monticello* encountered a violent storm and sank five miles off Yarmouth Cape, en route from Saint John to Yarmouth. Forty-six lives were lost, making it one of Yarmouth's greatest shipping tragedies — leaving fifteen widows and forty-nine fatherless children. The ship was owned by the Yarmouth Steamship Company.

The paddle steamer City of Monticello.

November 11th

1918
Canadian soldier George Price died near Mons, Belgium — shot by a German sniper. He is believed to be the last Canadian soldier to die in the First World War — just two minutes before the armistice took effect at 11 a.m. He was born in Falmouth, NS, in 1892.

1929
Dedication of the First World War Cenotaph on the Grand Parade in Halifax took place. Prior to this, Remembrance Day services were held at the Boer War Memorial adjacent to Province House.

George Price.

NOVEMBER 12TH

Halifax Memorial Public Library.

1951
The Halifax Memorial Public Library was opened after six years of meetings and planning. It closed in August 2014 in preparation for the opening of the new downtown Halifax Central Library on the corner of Spring Garden Road and Queen Street. (Also see Halifax Central Library, December 13, 2014.)

NOVEMBER 13TH

1903
Thomas H. Raddall (1903–1994) was born in Hythe, Kent, England. He moved to Nova Scotia with his family at the age of ten. Later in life he resided in Liverpool.

Beginning in the early forties, he was an award-winning writer of a number of works on Nova Scotian history, notably *Halifax Warden of the North* (1948), and historical fiction, including *His Majesty's Yankees* (1942), *Roger Sudden* (1944), *Pride's Fancy* (1946), *The Nymph and the Lamp* (1950), *The Governor's Lady* (1960), *Hangman's Beach* (1966) and *In My Time, A Memoir* (1976). He died on April 1, 1994.

November 14th

1606

The *Order of Good Cheer* celebrated at Annapolis Royal. With its motto to offer "Fellowship and Good Cheer," the event included an outdoor theatrical performance written by Marc Lescarbot, a lawyer who had arrived in July. He called his play *Le Theatre de Neptune en la Nouvelle-France*. The play told the story of sailors travelling to the New World, only to encounter Neptune, God of the Sea and his Tritons. The play included a series of welcoming speeches by Mi'kmaq chiefs. Lescarbot later returned to France in 1607 and wrote about his travels, publishing *Histoire de la Nouvelle-France* in 1609. Neptune Theatre in Halifax is named after Lescarbot's play.

Order of Good Cheer — L'Ordre de Bon Temps, 1606, as envisaged by illustrator C.W. Jefferys in 1942.

November 15th

The Saint Antonios Antiochian Orthodox Church, Halifax.

Samuel Cunard.

2015

After three years of renovations, the Orthodox Lebanese community opened the new Saint Antonios Antiochian Orthodox Church. The community then launched the Lebanese Festival in Halifax in August 2002 to convey their thanks to fellow Nova Scotians.

1787

Sir Samuel Cunard (d. 1865) was born in Halifax. Cunard would go on to create the British and North American Royal Mail Steam-Packet Company (1839) and in 1879, the Cunard Steamship Company. The Cunard Line celebrated 175 years in 2015.

November 16th

1857
William Hall (1827–1904) won the Victoria Cross on this date for his action at the Siege of Lucknow — the first African Nova Scotian person to win the VC. At the time, Hall was with the Royal Navy, serving as captain of the foretop with the HMS *Shannon*. The British army's commanding officer of the Lucknow Residency during the siege, with the 32nd (Cornwall) Regiment of Foot, was Nova Scotian born Colonel John Inglis (1814–1862).

1843
Gabriel Anthony was confirmed as chief of the Mi'kmaq of Annapolis, Digby, Yarmouth, Shelburne, and Queens counties by letters patent under the Great Seal of Nova Scotia. He estimated the number of people "under his charge" at 500.

William Hall.

November 17th

1885
An important discovery of gold was made in Hants County. Gold was mined at Renfrew, Nova Scotia, near Nine Mile River. The village was the home of one of the largest gold mines in the province. There were other gold mines in the community of Rawdon Gold Mines.

November 18th

2003
The Deep Roots Music Cooperative Society was formed in the Annapolis Valley. Since their founding, the festival has organized an annual (late September) fall weekend program of concerts and workshops in Wolfville.

November 19th

2011
The Government of France announced that Nova Scotian Andrew John Bayly (A.J.B.) Johnston, Canadian historian and writer, would be made a Chevalier of the Ordre des Palmes Académiques in recognition of his body of work associated with the history of the Fortress of Louisbourg. Johnston authored fourteen books of history, over one hundred articles on different aspects of the history of Atlantic Canada, three novels of historical fiction, and wrote for many historical-themed exhibits.

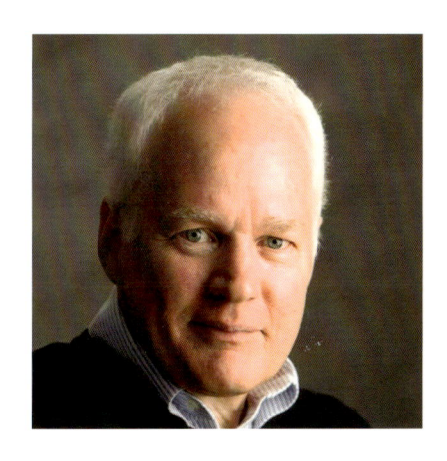

A.J.B. Johnston.

November 20th

1785
Governor Parr wrote in his letter to England that ". . . upwards of 25,000 Loyalists have already arrived in the Province, most of whom, with the exception of those who went to Shelburne, came to Halifax before they became distributed throughout the Province"

November 21st

2014
Robert (Bob) Manuge died at his family home in Lake Annis, Yarmouth County. He was ninety-three. He was instrumental in attracting Michelin Tire to establish plants in Nova Scotia in 1969. He later owned Manuge Galleries Ltd. in Halifax.

November 22nd

1753
Richard John Uniacke (d. 1830) was born in County Cork, Ireland. He was an abolitionist, lawyer, politician and eventually attorney general of Nova Scotia. He later fought in the Eddy Rebellion (also known as the Battle of Fort Cumberland, near the eventual border between Nova Scotia and New Brunswick), which was an effort to bring the American Revolution to Nova Scotia in late 1776. Uniacke was sent as a prisoner to Halifax. But through his connections, and for providing evidence for the Crown, he was released. He later stood for Catholic emancipation, founded the Charitable Irish Society, helped establish King's College and refused to legalize slavery in Nova Scotia. He advocated for the Confederation of Canada fifty-one years before it happened. His son, James Boyle Uniacke, would become the first Premier of Nova Scotia. (Also see James Boyle Uniacke, January 19, 1799.)

Richard John Uniacke, by Robert Field, 1811.

2006
John Allan Cameron died. Known as the "Godfather of Celtic Music," he was born in Inverness County, Cape Breton. He released his first album in 1968 and went on to release ten more in his career. He was a regular on the Halifax-based CBC program *Singalong Jubilee* in the 1960s (see Singalong Jubilee, July 3, 1961). He later had his own program, *The John Allan Cameron Show*, produced with CTV in Montreal. It moved to CBC Halifax in 1979 till 1981. He was made a Member of the Order of Canada in 2003.

John Allan Cameron, Boston, Massachusetts, on April 18, 1990.

November 23rd

1960
Muriel Duckworth, Peggy Hope-Simpson and other interested women began to organize a Nova Scotia Chapter of the Voice of Women (VOW) for Peace in Halifax. On December 7, 1960, a large public meeting was held at the Sir Charles Tupper School where Halifax women were encouraged to join the peace movement. Largely motivated by the collapse of the Paris peace talks that had taken place on May 16 (after a US spy plane, U-2, was shot down over Soviet airspace), they formed an action group and a study group and participated in various VOW international conferences. Many VOW women went on to form and participate in the New Democratic Party of Nova Scotia.

1950
Jeremiah 'Jerry' Alvin Jones died (born in Truro, 1858). A First World War veteran who served with the 106th Battalion (NS Rifles) in the Canadian Expeditionary Forces, he had lied about his age, saying he was thirty-nine, when he was actually fifty-eight. He was later recommended for the Distinguished Conduct Medal at the Battle of Vimy Ridge, but there was no record of his having received it — it was granted posthumously as the Canadian Forces Medallion for Distinguished Service on February 22, 2010. Jerry was the grandfather of well-known social activist Rocky Jones. (Also see Rocky Jones, July 29, 2013.)

Jeremiah 'Jerry' Alvin Jones.

November 24th

1839
William Eager died at the age of forty-three (born in Ireland in 1796). A businessman, artist and teacher, he arrived in Halifax from St. John's, Newfoundland, in 1834. In 1838, he organized a major art exhibition in Halifax featuring his work and the work of his students, representing over 125 items. In July and August of 1839, he published his first lithographs in two parts, titled *Nova Scotia Illustrated.* Parts three and four were published posthumously in May and August 1840.

Halifax from the Eastern Passage, by William Eager, 1837.

November 25th

1982
Halifax Mayor Ron Wallace and Hakodate Mayor Yasushi Yano signed a twinning agreement between their similar cities — a busy port, a historic star-shaped citadel and a northerly climate. In 2017, the thirty-fifth anniversary of the agreement, Mayor Mike Savage met with Hakodate's mayor, Toshiki Kudo, and various delegates on July 12.

November 26th

1921
The first public event was held at the newly built King's Theatre in Annapolis Royal (formerly the Bijou Dream Theatre, which had fallen victim to a fire). The Honourable George Murray, Premier of Nova Scotia, spoke at a political rally hosted at the theatre.

November 27th

1784
Brook Watson (1735–1807) was appointed agent for Nova Scotia in London. Watson came to Nova Scotia as a young boy and soon began trading, achieving success as a merchant by supplying provisions to the British military (serving under Wolfe) and engaging in business in London, Montreal and Boston. In London, he became a member of the original committee of the Corporation of Lloyd's of London in 1772, and later an alderman and then Lord Mayor of London in 1796 and a director of the Bank of England.

November 28th

1976
Mona Leonhardt Foster (née Parsons) died in Wolfville (b. 1901). She grew up in Wolfville and was educated at the Acadia Ladies' Seminary and later in Boston, where she became an actress for a brief time. She trained as a nurse, but soon married a Dutch businessman, Willem Leonhardt, and moved to Holland. After the German invasion of Holland in May 1940, she and her husband became members of an informal resistance network in the Netherlands from 1940 to 1941. She was arrested at her home on September 29, 1941 — the only Canadian female civilian to be imprisoned by the Nazis for helping downed Allied airmen escape. She was tried by a Nazi military tribunal, found guilty of treason and sentenced to death by firing squad. However, her sentence was appealed and was commuted to life with hard labour. She escaped in March 1945 as Allied forces bombed the prison camp, walking for three weeks across northern Germany and back to Holland. She was able to meet up with Canadian troops — ironically, the North Nova Scotia Highlanders. She returned to Nova Scotia in 1956.

Wolfville native Mona Parsons.

November 29th

1949

Stan Rogers was born in Ontario, but many Nova Scotians considered him one of their own, as his parents had deep roots in Guysborough County — a place where he spent many summers as a boy. He had a love for music from a young age, receiving his first guitar from an uncle when he was five years old. He played a twelve-string guitar during his many performances. He became known for his rich and passionate singing voice and for his finely crafted songs that harkened back to another time, including "Barrett's Privateers", "The Mary Ellen Carter", "Northwest Passage" and many more. Rogers died tragically on June 2, 1983, on an Air Canada flight that made an emergency landing in Cincinnati due to a smoke-filled cabin. He and twenty-two other passengers succumbed to smoke inhalation.

Stan Rogers.

November 30th

2007

Cape Breton University commemorated the fiftieth anniversary of the Beaton Institute, or "Cape Bretoniana," as it was known back in junior college days. The institute began in 1957 under the leadership of Sister Margaret Beaton (1893–1975) when, after returning from studies at Edinburgh University in Scotland, she had been encouraged to start a regional collection of Scottish and Gaelic materials pertaining to Cape Breton Island. The institute was later home to a vast print, visual and audio history collection relating to Cape Breton's rich culture, history and diverse heritage, including Mi'kmaq, African Nova Scotian, Jewish, Scottish, Gaelic, Acadian, Ukrainian, Lithuanian, Polish and Italian communities. The institute also housed over 60,000 images dating from the mid-nineteenth century.

1968

A meeting was held to discuss the creation of an organization to advocate for the black community in Nova Scotia. On August 15, 1969, with funding support from the federal government, the Black United Front (BUF) was created. Jules Oliver became its first executive director.

December

December 1st

1997
The Honourable Justice K. Peter Richard released his Westray Public Enquiry report, which stated in part that "The Westray Story . . . is . . . of incompetence, of mismanagement, of bureaucratic bungling, of deceit, of ruthlessness, of cover-up, of apathy, of expediency, and of cynical indifference. It is a tragic story, with the inevitable moments of pathos and heroism . . . an event that, in all good common sense, ought not to have occurred. It did occur and that is our unfortunate legacy."(Also see: At 5:18 a.m., May 9, 1992.)

2016
From December 1 to 3, the second annual Bluenose Ability Film Festival (BAFF), Canada's first and only disability film festival, took place in Halifax during the United Nations' International Day of Persons with Disabilities.

December 2nd

College Hall, Acadia University.

1877
The first College Hall at Acadia University burned to the ground.

1730
The Great Seal of the Province of Nova Scotia was authorized — the first of its kind in Canada.

December 3rd

Honourable Geoff Regan.

2015
The Honourable Geoff Regan became the first Nova Scotian Speaker of the House of Commons in almost a century (the Honourable Edgar Nelson Rhodes from Amherst had served as Speaker from 1917 to 1922). He also became the chief administrative officer of the House and oversaw all financial and administrative matters concerning the operations of the House of Commons and its 1,500 employees.

December 4th

Joseph Howe statue at Province House.

1904
The Joseph Howe statue at Province House was unveiled by Sir Charles Parsons. It was designed by Quebec sculptor Louis-Phillippe Hébert (1850–1917). Sir Charles Parsons was considered one of the greatest British engineers of his age (1854–1931). He had established the Parsons Marine Steam Turbine Company in 1897 and held over 300 patents.

December 5th

1884
The SS *Newcastle* sailed from Halifax to Britain with a large cargo of Annapolis Valley apples. This was the middle of the apple boom (1849–1933).

December 6th

1985
Daniel Paul, Mi'kmaw elder, columnist, author and human rights activist (b. 1938 at Indian Brook) became the founding executive director of the Confederacy of Mainland Mi'kmaq at the Millbrook Reserve in Truro. He remained in that role till January 1994. He had previously worked for the federal and provincial governments. In 1991, he also founded and published the *Mi'kmaq/Maliseet Nations News.* Paul served on the NS Human Rights Commission, the NS Police Commission and authored *We Were Not Savages* (1993). He was named to the Order of Nova Scotia in 2002, and the Order of Canada in November 2005.

December 6th (cont'd)

Lunenburg waterfront.

1995
Old Town Lunenburg was listed as a UNESCO World Heritage Site, as one of the best surviving examples of a planned British colonial settlement in North America, established in 1753. It was listed as a "National Historic District" in 1992 by the federal government. On August 16, 1996, the distinctive UNESCO monument commemorating the official designation of Lunenburg as a World Heritage Site was unveiled in Lunenburg.

Looking south along the railway track after the explosion.

1917
The Halifax Explosion occurred, resulting from a collision between the SS *Mont-Blanc*, carrying highly flammable and explosive materials, and the Norwegian vessel SS *Imo* in the Halifax Harbour. The explosion devastated the Tufts Cove and Turtle Grove areas in Dartmouth, and the Richmond and North End districts of Halifax. Two thousand people were killed, 9,000 injured and 20,000 were left homeless. Halifax's population at that time was 55,000.

December 7th

The popular Trailer Park Boys, *John Tremblay (Julian), Robb Wells (Ricky) and Mike Smith (Bubbles) teamed up with OrganiGram in 2016 to create their very own weed brand.*

2001

The Nova Scotia–based Canadian mockumentary television series *Trailer Park Boys* premiered on Showcase. Directed by Mike Clattenburg, the series follows the shady exploits of Ricky (Robb Wells), Julian (John Paul Tremblay) and "Bubbles" (Mike Smith). The series ran on Showcase till 2007, and was later revived on Netflix. In November 2016, it was announced that the Canadian licensed producer of medical cannabis, OrganiGram, based in Moncton, New Brunswick, had officially partnered with TPS productions, a company owned by none other than Wells, Tremblay and Smith, to create their very own weed brand.

December 8th

1948

The Maritime Museum of Canada was established in Halifax. Initially located at the HMC Dockyard (and later renamed the Maritime Museum of the Atlantic), it moved through several locations before its own building was constructed in 1981 as part of a waterfront redevelopment program. In 1982, the museum received the CSS *Acadia*. It is the oldest and largest maritime museum in Canada.

December 9th

1755

The first post office was established in Halifax (the first in what later became Canada).

December 10th

2008

Sambro resident and playwright Catherine Banks won a Governor General's Literary Award for English-language Drama for her play *Bone Cage*. She won a second award in 2012 for *It is Solved by Walking*. She was born in Middleton and graduated from Acadia University. She has remarked that ". . . it really wasn't until I saw Michel Tremblay's *Les Belles Soeurs* that I understood that I had something to write about . . . Tremblay characters were so grounded in real life that I understood that I had lots to write. I have said many times that the first time I sat down and wrote dialogue I felt I had come home."

Catherine Banks of Halifax, winner of the 2008 award for English-language Drama, received a specially bound copy of her Bone Cage, *from Her Excellency the Right Honourable Michäelle Jean, twenty-seventh governor general of Canada.*

1954

The last load of fill was dumped on the Strait of Canso. The causeway construction required over 1,385 metres of rock-fill, in waters of a maximum depth of 65 metres. The official opening took place on August 13, 1955. The word Canso was believed to be derived from the Mi'kmaq word *kamsok*, which meant "opposite the lofty cliffs."

1957

Argyris Lacas died in Halifax, age one hundred (b. 1856 in Greece). He was a prominent member of a generation of Halifax Greeks, and a small-business owner for many years.

December 11th

1902

A great banquet was held at the Queen Hotel for the Honourable W.S. Fielding. Fielding was the Minister of Finance for Canada, and the dinner was hosted by the Liberal Party of Nova Scotia, on the occasion of Fielding's return from England, where he had been one of the representatives of Canada at the Coronation of His Majesty King Edward VII and attended the Colonial Conference in London.

Honourable W.S. Fielding and family.

December 12th

1989
Helen Creighton died (b. Sept. 5, 1899). Born in Dartmouth, she was a journalist broadcaster (on CHNS as 'Aunt Helen') and became a distinguished folklorist, collecting numerous songs and stories across Nova Scotia, and recording and publishing works from 1928 onwards. In 1932, she published her first book, *Songs and Ballads of Nova Scotia*. Though there are different perspectives about her work, she played a key role in shaping the contemporary Nova Scotian identity. She was recognized with numerous honorary degrees, a fellowship in the American Folklore Society and the Order of Canada for her contributions to cultural history. In 2001, Nova Scotia writer and producer Donna Davies released a 73 min. documentary on Creighton entitled *A Sigh and A Wish: Helen Creighton's Maritimes*.

Helen Creighton.

December 13th

The Halifax Central Library.

2014
The new Halifax Central Library opened on the corner of Spring Garden Road and Queen Street. The library won a Lieutenant Governor's Design Award in Architecture for 2014. The design was a joint venture between local firm Fowler Bauld and Mitchell and Schmidt Hammer Lassen of Denmark. The total cost of the building was $57.6 million.

1804
Joseph Howe was born, the last of eight children. (Also see John Howe, December 28, 1780.)

December 14th

1917

Group of Seven artist Arthur Lismer, the director of the Victoria School of Art and Design in Halifax (1916 to 1919), wrote to the curator of the Art Gallery of Toronto concerning the damages caused at his school in the Halifax Explosion on December 6, but concludes, "Now all these are small things compared with the awful damage and death toll in the devastated area, that is indeed a woeful sight — and our 20,000 homeless (we are all caring for them) & the numerous blinded people — & the little children — a sight of any of these would depress the tenderest soul . . . my school is full of coffins now & all boarded up." (Also see: The Halifax Explosion, December 6, 1917.)

Where the Five Fisherman's Restaurant was later located. The Victoria School of Art and Design was on the top two floors above the Fleischmann Yeast Company. The school stored these coffins during preparations to bury the dead from the Halifax Explosion.

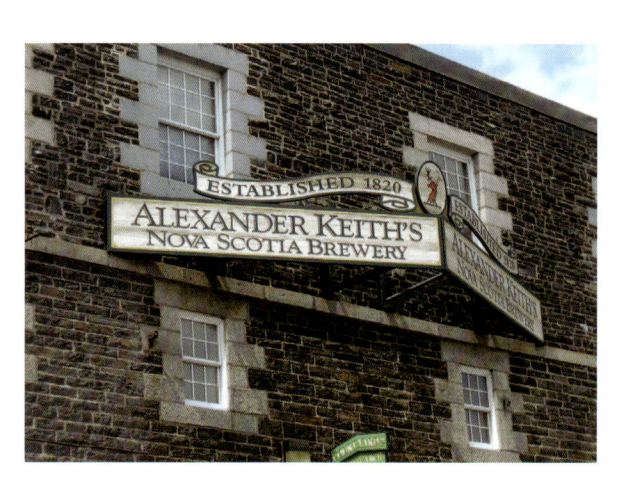

1873

Alexander Keith died. He was a noted Scottish-born Canadian politician (Conservative), freemason and brewer. In 1820, he founded the Alexander Keith's Nova Scotia Brewery. He was buried in the Camp Hill Cemetery, where his birthday on October 5 (1795), was often marked by people visiting the grave and placing beer bottles and caps on it.

Alexander Keith's Building, Halifax.

December 15th

1902
Guglielmo Marconi (1874–1937) sent wireless signals across the Atlantic from Table Head, Glace Bay, to Britain. The first official transatlantic message was from Governor General Minto to King George V. In 1909, Marconi received the Nobel Prize in Physics.

Table Head, Glace Bay, the site where Guglielmo Marconi sent the first wireless signals across the Atlantic to Britain.

1985
Frank Sobey died (b. 1902). Born in Lyons Brook, Nova Scotia, he left school after Grade 8. With a focused entrepreneurial spirit he expanded his father's meats and vegetables store in Stellarton to a full range of groceries. Soon he expanded to New Glasgow, Antigonish and further afield, creating a holding company called Empire Company Ltd., encompassing substantial commercial and residential real estate holdings and other services. Sobey also created a foundation to provide funding supports to a wide range of health, education and community based initiatives. Over the years, he amassed a significant art collection, and the foundation's Sobey Art Award remained Canada's largest prize for young Canadian artists.

1868
Thomas Killam died (b. 1802), a prominent Yarmouth merchant (trade and insurance), a ship-owner and politician. Between 1839 and 1865 he owned over sixty vessels, twenty-five of which were eventually lost at sea. He entered politics as an MLA for the Township of Yarmouth in 1847, serving for twenty years. In 1867, he was elected as an MP to the first Parliament.

December 16th

1757
John Connor died at age twenty-nine, and was buried in the Old Burial Ground in Halifax. He arrived in Nova Scotia in 1749 as a volunteer settler with Edward Cornwallis' fleet on the ship *Merry Jacks*. Mi'kmaq oral tradition recorded that Connor's pregnant wife, Mary, and his daughter Martha were killed in a raid on Dartmouth in 1751.

John Connor (1728–1757), Old Burial Ground, Halifax.

December 17th

1997
Alma Bardon Houston died in Halifax (b. in Stewiacke, 1926). She was known as the "first lady of Inuit art." She and her son, filmmaker John Houston, ran the Houston North Gallery in Lunenburg, specializing in Inuit art. She had extensive experience with the Inuit artists of Baffin Island and Cape Dorset for many years. She also began to encourage local enterprise initiatives and was an instrumental supporter in the founding of the Lunenburg Folk Harbour Festival Society in 1986. Commenting on his mother, John observed, "My mother was the single human being in the world who had the longest daily contact with Inuit art." According to her wishes, John and his brother, Sam, scattered her ashes in the hills above Cape Dorset.

December 18th

1603
Pierre Dugua des Mons (Monts) received letters patent and, " . . . was granted the privilege of trade and responsibility of settlement by the king. Under the terms of his commissions, he was given a trading monopoly and appointed lieutenant-general 'of the coasts, lands and confines of Acadia, Canada and other places in New France,' there to establish 60 colonists a year and to win the Indians to the Christian faith."

December 19th

1843
The Christmas classic *A Christmas Carol Featuring Ebenezer Scrooge* by Charles Dickens was published in England in a single volume. A year earlier, Dickens had been hosted in Halifax by Joseph Howe (See Joseph Howe, Jan. 21, 1842). Dickens's first edition sold out by Christmas Eve and by the end of 1844 thirteen editions had been released.

December 20th

1764
A large tract of country upon the southeast side of the Piziquid River (later known as the Avon River) was erected into a township to be called Windsor. It was formerly known as Pisiquit, where Fort Edward was built (1750) during Father Le Loutre's War (1749–1755), and where the site of the Acadian church for the parish of l'Assumption (est. 1722) was located.

December 21st

1941
Butter rationing began in Canada as a wartime measure. Gasoline had been rationed since April 1.

December 22nd

1835
George Monro Grant was born in Stellarton, Pictou County (d. 1902). Educated at the Pictou Academy, and later in Scotland at the University of Glasgow, he entered the ministry of the Church of Scotland, serving at St. Matthew's Church in Halifax. In favour of Confederation, in 1872 he accompanied his lifelong friend, Sir Sandford Fleming, on a railway survey expedition to assess the best route through the Rockies, producing a best-selling book from the trip called *Ocean to Ocean* (1873). He became principal of Queen's College (later University) in Kingston, Ontario (1877).

George Monro Grant.

December 23rd

NSCR steam engine that ran on the Nictaux line.

1889
Nictaux Atlantic (the Nova Scotia Central Railway — NSCR) opened its railway line between Middleton and Bridgewater.

December 24th

1942
The HMCS *Clayoquot* was torpedoed by German U-boat U-806 three miles off the Sambro Lighthouse. The ship sank in ten minutes, with eight men lost. Seventy-six who abandoned the ship were recovered and taken ashore.

December 25th

2004
Mi'kmaq Kji-Keptin (Grand Captain) Alexander Denny died (b. 1940). He served as president of the Union of Nova Scotia Indians from 1974 to 1976 and from 1993 to 1995. He was a lifetime member of the Mi'kmaq Santé Mawio'mi (Grand Council).

December 26th

1925
Canadian labour leader Robert Drummond died in Stellarton, and was buried in Springhill (b. 1840 in Scotland). He was a coal miner, trade union leader, journalist and politician. Ian McKay wrote that Drummond was, ". . . one of the most significant figures of 19th-century Canadian labour history . . . For all his contradictions, inconsistencies, and reversals, and perhaps partly because of them, Drummond, was one of Nova Scotia's more interesting new liberal politicians, should also be remembered as a representative and revealing figure in Canadian working-class history."

1932
The Islamic Association of Nova Scotia was formally established. It was one of the first Muslim organizations in Canada. A Maritime Muslim Academy was founded in 1984 in the Halifax/Dartmouth area. A new Ummah mosque and community centre in Halifax was granted final occupancy in May of 2013.

December 27th

1883
Cyrus Eaton was born in Pugwash (d. 1979). He became a successful Canadian-American investment banker, businessman and philanthropist, with a career spanning over seventy years. He had a passion for world peace and was an outspoken critic of the Cold War, establishing the Pugwash conferences at his summer home in Pugwash, NS, to encourage international dialogue. The conferences and their chairman, Joseph Rotblat, received the Nobel Peace Prize in 1995.

Thinkers' Lodge, Pugwash, Nova Scotia.

1932
Peter Wilmot died at the age of 106 on the Millbrook Reserve (born at Pictou Landing in 1826). He was a Mi'kmaw chief at Pictou Landing.

December 28th

John Howe (1754–1835) by William Valentine (NB Museum).

1780
The Halifax Journal was founded by John Howe (1754–1835). He arrived in Halifax the previous year. He had witnessed the Boston Tea Party in December 1773 and considered himself a Loyalist — not so much to the Crown, but rather to the "British heritage, and the contribution of Britons over the centuries to politics, the arts, science, and literature." Before evacuating to Halifax, he had trained as a junior partner on two Boston newspapers. He was the father of Joseph Howe (1804–1873). (Also see Howe, January 14, 1851.)

1979
Premier John Buchanan's Conservative government passed its multi-plant *Trade Union Act* amendment in the Nova Scotia Legislature, later known as the Michelin Bill, that required the simultaneous signing of workers from all "interdependent" plants. This was retroactive and made the previous application for union certification, which was conducted in October at the Michelin Granton plant, null and void. The results of the Granton plant vote were never known and the *Act* effectively stopped the unionization of Michelin.

December 29th

1923
John Frederic Herbin died in Wolfville (b. 1860 in Windsor). He was an author, poet, historian, politician and jeweller. He learned the jewellry and watchmaker trade under his father, and by 1885 he established Herbin Jewellers in Wolfville, where he spent the rest of his life (the business continued after his death). He was mayor of Wolfville from 1902 to 1903. He was the author of *Canada and Other Poems* (1891), *The Marshlands* (1893), *Grand Pré* (1898), *The Heir to Grand Pré* (1907) and *Jen of the Marshes* (1921). Literary historian Gwendolyn Davies observed that Herbin was " . . . a torch keeper of the Acadian past through his literary work and his endeavours to promote a park at Grand Pré . . . most effectively contributed to the nation-building spirit of both Acadians and Canadians during his lifetime." (Also see National Historic Site, June 30, 2012.)

December 30th

1938
Lee (Harvey) Cremo was born at Barra Head, Chapel Island, Cape Breton (d. Oct. 10, 1999). He grew up in Eskasoni and started playing the fiddle at the age of seven, later taking lessons from his father, Simon Peter Cremo (1900–1964). Lee became a famed fiddler and composer, who won over eighty fiddle competitions. He was remembered as an ambassador for the Cape Breton Mi'kmaq community.

1816
William Alexander Henry was born in Halifax. He was a delegate to the Charlottetown Conference and was considered a Father of Confederation. He later became mayor of Halifax (1870). He was also one of the first judges of the Supreme Court of Canada, appointed in 1875. The well-known restaurant and pub in Halifax, Henry House, served as his residence from 1854 to 1864. He died in Ottawa in 1888.

December 31st

The Halifax Armoury, 1899.

1898
After three years of construction work, the Halifax Armoury (and Drill Hall) was completed. The building was designed by Chief Dominion Architect Thomas Fuller (1823–1898). J.E. Askwith Co. of Ottawa was the contractor, with an original cost estimate of $175,000, but the project went over-budget at a final cost of about $250,000, which was considered an astronomical sum. Fuller was also one of the principal architects (with Charles Baillargé) who designed the Parliament building (completed in 1866). The Armoury was considered one of the most advanced structures of its day, creating a large interior space with no columns or walls — it is one of the oldest surviving examples of such a building design. It was also one of the first buildings in Halifax to be lit by electricity. The Armoury was associated with the Princess Louise Fusiliers, formed in 1869, who saw action in the Riel Rebellion, the South African War and both World Wars. It was formally recognized as a National Historic Site on June 22, 1989.

Photo Credits

Acadia University Alumni: 152
Acadia University Archives: 108
A.C.Fine Art Inc.: 120
Africvillemuseum.org: 44
Ajbjohnston.com: 169
Allmusic.com: 146
Annapolis Heritage Society Archives: 58
Annemurraycentre.com: 38
Appleblossom.com: 101
Art Gallery of Nova Scotia: Back Cover, Table of Contents, 9, 11, 19, 54, 62, 99, 130, 121, 125, 138, 147, 151, 171
Art Gallery of Ontario: 106
Atlantic.ctvnews.ca: 160
Authentic Seacoast Company: 45
Bank of Canada: 8
Beaton Institute Digital Archives: 163
Bestphotos83.blogspot.ca: 111
Biographi.ca: 163
BIO Newsletter: 165
Blackcanadianpoetry.com: 81
Black Cultural Centre for Nova Scotia: 118, 120
Blackhistorycanada.ca, Nova Scotia Office of the Lieutenant Governor: 141
Bold Privateers, Roger Marsters: 94, 97
British Library: 182
Canada Council for the Arts, with permission from:
    Martin Lipman: 54
    P. Doyle: 178
Canadian House of Commons Collection: 70
Canadian Museum of History: 87
Canadian Virtual War Memorial: 166
Canadian War Museum: 70
Cape Breton at the Beginning of the Twentieth Century, C.W. Vernon: 30
Cape Breton Miners' Museum: 125
Capebretonpost.com: 85
Cbc.ca: 35, 173
    Photographer, Geoff D'Eon: 104
CB Wireless Heritage Society: 181
Centre for Newfoundland Studies, Memorial University: 119
Chinesecanadian.ubc.ca, Albert Lee: 132
Chronicle Herald: 51, 75
City of Vancouver Archives: 154

Clga.ca: 149
Collections Canada: 59
Communications Nova Scotia: Back Cover, Table of Contents, 85, 143, 157
Cwjefferys.ca: 168
Dalhousie University Alumni: 13
Dalhousie Medical Alumni Association: 82
Dalhousie University Killam Library Special Collections: 143
Deafculturecentre.ca: 127
Department of National Defense: 77
Destination Cape Breton Association: 114
Destination Halifax: 23
Dusan Kadlec: 56
First to Die, Bryan Elson: 157
Flickr, Paul Asman and Jill Lenoble: 10
Fortress Halifax, Mike Parker: 156
Gay.hfxns.org: 141
Glenn Loxdale, with thanks to the Africville Heritage Trust: Cover, 17
GreatWarAlbum.ca: 75
Gwen North: 7, 113 , 180
Halifaxartmap.com: 139, 147
Halifax A Visual Legacy, William Naftel: 37, 53, 71, 185, 148 156
Halifaxhistory.ca: 159
Halifax's Northwest Arm, Heather Watts and Michele Raymond: 87, 131
Halifax: The First 250 Years, Judith Fingard, Janet Guildford, and David Sutherland: 21, 23, 40, 65, 79, 99, 103, 109, 110, 142, 144, 145, 167, 168, 184
Halifaxwomenshistory.ca: 46
Harold A Skaarup: 8
Historic Annapolis Valley, Mike Parker: 106
Historicplaces.ca: 121
Historymuseum.ca: 81
HMHPS.ca: 160
Howarddill.com: 96
Hulton Archive/Getty Images: 66
iStock: Cover, 12
Jeff Vienneau: 176
John Cabot & The Voyage of the Matthew, Brian Cutherbertson: 110
Johngracie.ca: 72
Journal.lib.uoguelph.ca: 98

Ken Eckert: 29
Kent Nason: 26
Kings County Museum: 160
Leo J. Deveau: 22, 28, 102, 136, 137, 140, 168
Lestroispignons.com: 153
Library.acadiau.ca: 174
Library and Archives Canada: 20, 36, 68, 72, 122, 124, 127, 129, 128, 138, 140, 147
Library and Archives Canada, Duncan Cameron: 116
Louisburg: A Living History Colourguide, Susan Young de Biagi: 29
Lunenburg Art Gallery: 117
MacMaster Music Inc: 6, 107
Marieke Walsh: 107
Marinecurator.blogspot.ca: 41
McCord Museum, Notman Studios: 137
Menofthedeeps.com: 128
National Gallery of Canada: Back Cover, Table of Contents, 73, 89, 158
National Portrait Gallery, London: 45
News1130.com (©THE CANADIAN PRESS/HO-Nova Scotia Courts): 24
NewScotland1398.ca: 12
Niniskamijinaqik / Ancestral Images, Ruth Holmes Whitehead: 150
Nova Scotia Archives: Cover,14, 26, 35, 42, 48, 55, 60, 61, 64, 66, 74, 75, 79, 80, 84, 87, 89, 90, 92, 102, 104, 106, 117, 129, 134, 139, 157, 158, 161, 164, 165, 166, 176,178, 179, 180, 181, 184
Nova Scotia House of Assembly: 69
Nova Scotia Legislative Library: 51, 115, 155
    With permission from:
    Communications Nova Scotia: 49, 51
    James MacNutt: 50, 119
Nova Scotia Museum: 77, 170
Nscc.cairnrepo.org: 141
NS Museum of Industry: 16, 24, 78
Office of the Governor General of Canada: 47
Onens.ca: 55
OrganiGram, Facebook: Back Cover, 177

Parks Canada:
    Fort Anne Collection, Annapolis Royal: 95
    Halifax Citadel: 100
Pier21.ca: 34
Plate 31, Historical Atlas of Canada, R. Cole Harris and Geoffrey J. Matthews: 105
Policyalternatives.ca: 5, 112
Rankin Family Inc: 18
Remembering Singalong Jubliee, Ernest Dick: 115
Rnsys.com: 97
Royal NS Historical Society: 150
Sailmeom.com: 82
Saintantonios.ca: 159
Samuel Cunard: Nova Scotia's Master of the North Atlantic, John Boileau: 133
Sawkil.com: 125
Sfx Archives: 10
Socan.ca: 77
Stephen Archibald: 71
Stephen Swan: 9
The Artists' Halifax, Mora Dianne O'Neill: 54, 111, 112, 135, 142
The Bell Family in Baddeck, Judith Tullock, courtesy of Library of Congress: 43
Thecanadianencyclopedia.ca: Cover, 6, 33, 123
The Charles Macdonald House of Centerville Society: 67
The Coast, photographer:
    Krista Comeau: 31
    Robin Metcalfe: 163
The Evangeline Land, Amos Lawson Hardy: 151
The Gilder Lehrman Institute of American History: 91
The Halifax and Southwestern Railway Museum Lunenburg: 183
The Halifax Examiner: 78
The Hants Journal: 51
Theshipslist.com: 64
The South Shore Genealogical Society: 162
The Spirit of Africville: 44
Thevanguard.ca: 131
Trinity Historical Society Archives: 59
Triplet Records: 52
Tod Scott: 149
Torontodreamsproject.blogspot.ca: 32
Tourism Nova Scotia: Cover, Back Cover, Table of Contents, 11, 63, 108, 116, 123, 131
University Archives/US Historical Manuscripts: 132
View902.com: 74
Wartime Halifax, William D. Neftel: 4, 25, 142
Wartimeheritage.com: 57
Wikipedia Creative Commons: Cover, 4, 15, 21, 30, 37, 43, 53, 56, 78, 83, 86, 93, 94, 98, 101, 118, 126, 127, 135, 136, 146, 152, 153, 162, 169, 170, 171, 172, 174, 175, 179
    Photographers: Brian L. Burke: 100, Dennis Jarvis: 145
World Digital Library: 95
Yarmouth County Museum: 166
Youtube: 5, 39, 90, 96
Zwicker's Art Gallery: Cover, 27, 147

A NOTE ON SOURCES

As with Shirley Elliott's *Nova Scotia Book of Days*, the sources for this work include a vast array of primary and secondary sources.

Some of the most basic sources originate from such early works as Thomas Akins's *The History of Halifax* (1847), Beamish Murdoch's *A History of Nova Scotia, or Acadie* (1865–1867), and numerous excerpts from letters, speeches and diaries from such historical figures as Joseph Howe, Simeon Perkins, John Salusbury, Thomas Chandler Haliburton and many more.

Other extensive sources include both visual and textual references from the Nova Scotia Archives (NSARM), the Nova Scotia Museum (NSM), the Museum of Industry, Parks Canada, the Beaton Institute, the Black Loyalist Heritage Centre, the Africville Museum and the Yarmouth County Museum; the textual collections of the Royal Nova Scotia Historical Society, the journal writings at Acadiensis, the extensive web primary and secondary resources on Archive.org, CBC.ca, The Canadian Encyclopedia/Historica, Wikipedia.org, Library and Archives Canada, the online Dictionary of Canadian Biography (DCB); many of our province's university archives' sites and various historical works published by Formac Publishing and Nimbus Publishing; the Mi'kmaw Book of Days hosted online at Cape Breton University and other related Mi'kmaw history web sites; the Nova Scotia Legislative Library online resources, and the Lieutenant Governor of Nova Scotia web site, for their extensive historical reference links; and, lastly, the Art Gallery of Nova Scotia (AGNS).

If readers see that I've created an incorrect entry, or missed something of critical importance, I would like to hear about it for future online updates c/o 400years@formac.ca.

INDEX

4th Estate (newspaper) 78

A

abolitionism 17, 36, 55, 120, 170
Aboriginal Achievement Award *see* awards, Aboriginal Achievement
Academy of Music *see* music, Academy of
Acadia Coal Company 16
Acadian
    community 35, 73, 98, 131
    deportation 5, 94, 113, 140
    history 10, 36, 105, 113, 148, 149, 163, 173
    (re)settlement 5, 135, 152
Acadian (newspaper) 10
Acadia University 20, 27, 86, 98, 108, 147, 155, 174
accessibility legislation 83
Admiralty House 8
Aerial Experiment Association 42
African Americans 17, 71, 87, 118
African Canadians 13, 25, 118, 130, 144, 155, 158
African Diaspora Association of the Maritimes 59
African Heritage Month 27
African Nova Scotians
    in the arts 81, 144
    education 16, 55, 108, 155
    military 25, 83, 106, 108, 118
    notable 33, 55, 87, 98, 120, 123, 130, 139, 155
    music 17, 46
    politics 36, 55, 59, 60
    Sierra Leone 17
African School 15
African United Baptist Association 55
Africville 52, 87
    apology 44
    relocation 25, 52, 134, 151
airplanes 42, 90
Aix-la-Chapelle Treaty 113, 127
alcohol, sale of 19, 28, 81, 88, 133
Aldershot, NS 97
Alexander, William 5
Alline, Henry 69
Almon, William Johnston 40
American Revolution 62, 69, 91, 99, 139, 170
Amherst
    Jeffery 124
    Nova Scotia 78, 115
A. Murray MacKay Bridge 118
Angus L. MacDonald Bridge 65, 107, 118
Annapolis Royal, NS 27, 29, 58, 63, 95, 128, 135, 136, 140, 148, 168, 172
Annapolis Valley, NS 50, 101, 113, 133, 151, 175
Antigonish, NS 10, 48, 60
Aquash, Annie Mae 61
Archibald, Edith Jessie 91
Armstrong, Louis 159
Arrows Night Club 52
Art Gallery of Nova Scotia 125, 140, 147
artists 24, 36, 46, 54, 66, 78, 81, 84, 89, 104, 109, 117, 125, 133, 134, 136, 139, 147, 153, 171, 180, 181
Aspinquid, Saint (Mi'kmaq) 93
Association for the Advancement of Colored People (NS) 98
Asylum, Provincial Poor 164
Atlantic Advocate (newspaper) 64
Atlantic Insight (magazine) 64
Attack at Mocodome 41
Atwell, Yvonne 60
awards
    Aboriginal Achievement 69
    East Coast Music 72, 128
    Gemini 54
    Governor General's 13, 25, 26, 54, 102, 104, 123, 166, 178
    Juno 18, 32, 38, 43, 52

B

Baddeck, NS 121, 126
Bailly, Evern 'Earl' 117
Bank of Nova Scotia 21, 62, 124
Banks, Catherine 178
Barry, James Burns 109
Bartlett, Raymond 15
Basque, Elsie J. 73
Bateson, Nora 98
Battle of Beauséjour 94, 140
Battle of Grand Pré 36
Bay Ferries, Ltd. 73
Beaton Institute (Cape Breton U) 15, 173
Bedford-Sackville News (newspaper) 148
Belcher, Edward 47
Bell, Alexander Graham 20, 42, 121, 126
Bellevue House (Halifax) 53
Ben-Gurion, David 100
Benton, Catherine 24
Bernard, Ngema (Gena), life of 13
Berwick, NS 93
Best, Carrie 123
Big Pond, NS 77
Bill C-150 93
Birchtown, NS 17, 122, 139
Bird, Isabella, Lucy 111
Bird, Will R. 91
Black Cultural Centre for Nova Scotia 98
Black Loyalists 17, 27, 71, 122, 130
Black United Front 98, 173
Bland, James Fox 19
Blucke, Stephen 139
Bluenose
    Flying 128
    launch 61
    loss of 27, 61
    racing 159
    replica (*Bluenose II*) 61, 123
    see also Walters, Angus J.
Boat Harbour, pollution 21, 149
bootlegging *see* alcohol, sale of
Borden, Frederick 93
Borden, Robert 154
Boscawen, Edward 90, 91, 105, 124
Boudreau, Daniel 10
Boyd, George Elroy 25
Bras d'Or
    Biosphere Reserve 113
    Lake 42, 126
Bremner, James J. 72
bridges 21, 58, 65, 107, 118, 147
Bridgetown 50, 148
Bridgewater, NS 14, 155, 183
British Admiralty 12
British 5, 62, 94, 108
    French conflict 29, 63 68, 94, 105, 111, 127
    North American Act 62
    support from 16, 71, 108
    United States conflict 50, 62, 91
Bromley, Walter 16
Bruce, Harry 64, 88
Burying the Hatchet Ceremony 111
Bushell, John 59

C

Cabot, John 12, 110
Cabot Trail 12
Cameron, John Allan 170
Cameron, Silver Donald 78, 88
Camp Hill Cemetery 33, 116, 180
Canadian Bioscope Company 30
Canadian Broadcasting Company *see* CBC
Canadian Forces Base 91
Canso
    Causeway 93, 178
    Nova Scotia 68
Cape Breton
    causeway 93, 178
    Highland Links golf course 114
    Liberation Army 59
    music 13, 18, 32, 39 43, 128, 133, 153, 170
    people 10, 18, 35, 39, 42, 43, 80
    politics 13, 65, 69
    settlement of 5, 62, 63, 110, 132, 152
    steel plant closure 154
    Symphony Fiddlers 39
    University 21, 85, 173
Cape North, NS 110
Capitol Theatre (Halifax) 161
Carmelite Hermitage Nova Nada monastery 134
Carvery, Eddie 152
Castine expedition 136
CBC 35, 39, 54, 60, 89, 98, 100, 104, 115, 170
Celtic culture 19, 96, 146, 153, 170
Centreville, NS 67
Cerebus Rock 32
Chambers, Robert William 75
Champlain, Samuel de 46, 95, 98
Chapel Island, NS 126
Charles I 119
Charles Fort 5
Charlottetown Conference 138
Chebouctou *see* Chebucto Peninsula

Chebucto Peninsula 5, 58, 109
Chedabucto Bay 32
Chegoggin, NS 57
Cheticamp, NS 10, 153
Chiaisson, Anselme 10
Chinese community 132
Chipman Corner, NS 85
CHNS radio 90, 92, 104, 141, 179
choirs, provincial 17
Christmas, Ben 61
Christmas, Dan 160
Chronicle Herald (newspaper) 75, 79
Churchill, Winston 28, 142
Citadel, Halifax 136, 143, 156
citizenship 5
Civil Emergency Corps *see* Home Guard 25
Civil War, American 73, 106
Clare, NS 73
Clarke, George Elliott 13
Clarkson, John 17
Clayton, Custio 152
Coady, Moses 10
Coape Sherbrooke, John 136
coat of arms, provincial 21
Cobbett, William 103
Cohen, Nina 52, 125, 128
coinage 8
Colford, Wesley 59
Colville, Alex 120
Confederation 4, 21, 66, 71, 84, 114, 115, 140, 161, 185
Cook, James 91
Corning, Sara 57
Cornwallis
    district 102
    Edward 5, 109, 113, 119, 124, 127, 143, 148, 149, 181
Creighton, Helen 179
Creignish, NS 43
Crosby, Sydney 57
Cunard, Samuel 127, 133, 168
    ships 34, 41, 88, 111

D

Da Costa, Mathieu 95
Dalhousie
    Earl of 158
    Lord 99
Dalhousie University 13, 48, 50, 66, 83, 136, 142, 144, 152, 155, 166
    graduates 55, 73, 82, 140, 159
Dartmouth, NS 61, 87, 118, 149, 152
    Massacre 93
Davies, Thomas 94
Day, Foreshaw 89
Day, Judson Graham 85
Deaf, Halifax School for the 127
Deep Brook, NS 51
DeGarthe, William 37
democratic reform 5
Dennis, Agnes 80
Dennis, Clarissa (Clara) Archibald 46, 80
Denny, Grand Captain Alexander 183

Denny Jr., Grand Chief John 73
d'Eon, Désiré 35
DesBarres, J.F.W. 71, 129
Desmond, Viola 33, 98, 123, 141
Dexter, Darrell 62
DHX Media 96
Diamond Jubilee 110
Dickens, Charles 21, 182
Diefenbaker, John George 48
Digby, NS 51, 73, 155
Dill, Howard 96
Dingle Park (Halifax) 122, 131
disability film festival 174
Dominion Atlantic Railway Bridge 21
Dominion of Canada 114
Dominion Coal Company 30
Downey, Billy 52
Drummond Mine 65
Drummond, Robert 183
Duck Tolling Retriever 96
Duke of Kent 95
Dyott, William 130

E

earthquake 59
East Coast Music Awards *see* awards, East Coast Music
Eastern Front Theatre 25
East Mapleton 91
East Preston, NS 60, 87
Eaton, Cyrus 184
Elliott, Shirley 4, 155
Encounter on Urban Environment (conference) 42
d'Entremont, Simon 163
environmental pollution 21, 32
Eskasoni, NS 32, 73, 185
European settlement 5

F

Falmouth, NS 69, 129, 166
Feed Nova Scotia 112
feminism 82, 91, 127, 140, 141, 165
Fenery, Charles 105
Ferguson, Max 35
fiddling 39, 43, 107, 109, 133, 146 185
    festival of 13
Field, Robert 24, 45
film making 30, 54, 105
firsts
    African Nova Scotian 27, 55, 60, 87, 118, 130, 141, 144, 169
    airplanes 42, 90
    arts 84
    churches 71, 137
    coinage 8
    covered skating rink 9
    Governor General 47
    Historical Society 9
    hospital 58
    judiciary 24, 49, 130
    Mi'kmaq 24, 36, 73
    military 57, 137

    newspaper 9, 10, 16, 59
    politics 34, 141
    postal 81, 122, 177
    press, freedom 49
    provincial seal 174
    quintuplets 38
    radio 92
    railway 146
    schools 121
    streetcar 37
    synagogue 40
    tartan 51
    telegraph 15
    telephone 20
    women 24, 34, 36, 82, 120, 137, 140, 141, 157
First World War 4, 57, 70, 75, 78, 80, 91, 102, 108, 136, 151, 166, 171
fisheries, decline 10
Fitzgerald, Winston 'Scotty' 39
Fleming, Sandford 122, 131, 182
Forrestall, Tom 54
Fort Anne 29
Fortress Louisbourg 5, 29, 35, 45, 63, 65, 68, 90, 94, 97, 113, 124, 169
Fortune, Rose 27
Fox, Terry 87
Franchise Act 82
Francis, Mayann Elizabeth 141
Francis, Raymond 21
Francklin, Michael 93, 135
Free Schools Act 79
French settlers 5
Fuller, Alfred 16
Fuller Brush Company 16
Fuller, Thomas 58
Fyshe, Thomas 21

G

Gaelic culture 48, 96, 124, 145, 173
Gampo Abbey (monastery) 66
Gemini Award *see* awards, Gemini
George, David 17
Gesner, Abraham 85
Glace Bay, NS 19, 40, 52, 105, 106, 125, 152, 166, 181
Glooscap First Nation 119
Goldbloom, Ruth Miriam 137
Gorham College, fire 33
Gorham, James 33
Government House 143
Governor General's Award *see* awards, Governor General's
Grand Pré, NS 113, 116, 140
Grand Theatre (Halifax) 46
Grant, George Monro 182
Grant, John James 39
Gray, Jack L. 139
Great Depression 10
Great Village, NS 99
Greenwich, NS 108
Grigor, William 15
Group of Seven 32, 106

H

Haliburton, Thomas Chandler 115, 147
Halifax, NS
    airport 90
    Armoury 185
    Battle of 99
    bridges 65, 107, 118
    central library 179
    churches 11, 14, 45, 71, 78, 121
    Citadel 136
    Commons 118
    exhibitions 151
    Explosion 57, 77, 80, 105, 176, 180
    fires 48, 53, 71, 142, 164
    First World War 4, 166
    food bank 112
    gay and lesbian community 163
    Gottingen petition 69
    Greeks 178
    harbour 20, 32, 41, 58, 60, 119
    hospital 58
    incorporation 71
    Lord Nelson Hotel 157
    Mechanics' Institute 15, 155
    mosque 31
    Provisional Battalion 72
    Public Gardens 72, 146
    schools 15
    Seahorse Tavern 148
    settlement of 24, 109
    Sikh gurdwara 82
    synagogue 40
    telegraph 15, 42
    Town Clock 156
    twin city 172
    University of 66
    women's history 46, 79, 80, 137
    Yacht Club 97
Halifax Club 22
Halifax Gazette (newspaper) 59
Halifax Herald (newspaper) 9, 16, 80, 92, 140
Halifax Regional Municipality 64, 71
Hall, Gabriel 87
Hall, William 83, 169
Halliburton, Brenton 49, 56
Hamilton, Annie Isabella 82
Hamilton, Ross Douglas 149
Hantsport, NS 83, 106
Hardy, Amos Lawson 151
Harris, Lawren 106
Harvey, David Cobb 15
Henry, William Alexander 185
Herbert, Mary Eliza 120
Herbin, John Frederic 184
des Herbiers de la Ralière, Charles 113
Hicks, Henry 34, 50, 142
highways 76
HMCS *Haida* 57
HMS *Observer* 99
HMS *Shannon* 103
hockey 57, 92, 96, 138
Home Guard 25
Homem, Diogo 12

Hopson, Thomas Peregrine 113, 127
Horticulture, School of 14
Horton, NS 164
    Bluff 83, 116
hospital 58
House of Assembly 4, 48, 50, 65, 69, 135, 163
Howe, Joseph 10, 15, 16, 20, 21, 40, 49, 56, 58, 94, 116, 175, 179, 184
Huggins, Charles 147
Human Rights
    Commission (NS) 98
    Halifax Advisory Committee 134
Hutchinson, George Wylie 99

I

immigrants, schooling 16
immigration 4, 16, 34, 132
    Pier 21 23, 34, 137
Independent Labour Party 13
Indian Brook, NS 61
Inglis, Charles 45
Inverness, NS 107, 116, 170
Irving, shipbuilding 62
Islamic Association of Nova Scotia 183
Ivany Goals 55

J

Jackson, A.Y. 32
Jackson, Benjamin 106
James, Ron 152
Jean, Michaëlle 31
Jesuits 97
Jewish
    history 173
    military 100
    synagogues 40
    women 52
Joe, Rita 57
Joggins, NS 125
    Fossil Cliffs 116
Johnston, James W. (politician) 29
Jones, Burnley, 'Rocky' 124, 171
Jones, El 112
Jones, Jeremiah 'Jerry' Alvin 171
Jones, Lynn 155
Jones Bannerman, Frances 84
Juno Award *see* awards, Juno

K

Kadlec, Dusan 56
Kavanaugh, Lawrence 65
Keeler, Ruby 135
Keith, Alexander 180
Kejimkujik National Park 150
Kelly, Peter 44
Kempt, James 101
Kemptville, NS 101
Kentville, NS 34, 155
Killam, Thomas 181
King, Boston 17
King George III 69, 71, 112
King's College 33, 92, 138, 162
K'jipuktuk (Mi'kmaq) 5, 71, 109

Knockwood, Noel 69
Korean War 69

L

Lando, Anne 35
Langford, Samuel, life 15
Langstroth, Bill 89
Last Steps Memorial 136
Lebanese Nova Scotians 159, 168
LeBlanc, Hon. Arthur Joseph 39
LeFort, Elizabeth 153
Legge, Francis 116
Legislative Council, dissolution 19
Legislature, provincial 21, 34, 50, 65, 69
Leonhardt Foster, Mona 172
Leonowens, Anna Harriette 21, 137
Le Petit Courrier (newspaper) 35
LeRoy, Pierre 35
Lewis, Daurene Elaine 27
Lewis, Maud 9, 125
Liberal Party 34, 69, 75
libraries 98, 140, 167
    Garrison 136, 158, 160
    Halifax Central 179
Lismer, Arthur 32, 180
liquor, *see* alcohol, sale of
Little Lorraine, NS 89
Liverpool, NS 33, 90
Lonecloud, Jerry 24, 77
Longfellow, Henry Wadsworth 30
Louisbourg *see* Fortress Louisbourg
Lovitt, William D. 8
Lotz, James 'Jim' Robert 9
Lotz, Pat 9
Loyalists 5, 62, 71, 91, 152, 155, 170
    Black *see* Black Loyalists
Lunenburg, NS 89, 93, 104, 123, 130, 139, 146, 162, 176

M

Mabou, NS 18
MacAskill, Wallace R. 26
MacDonald, Angus L. 48, 75
    bridge 65
MacDonald, Charles 67
MacDonald, Flora 101
MacDonald, John A. 114
MacEachen, Allan J. 116
MacEwan, Paul 69
MacGillivray, Allister 19
MacGillivray, William D. 54
MacInnis, Rob 13
MacIsaac, Ashley 43
MacIvor, Daniel 123
Mackenzie, William Roy 38, 76
Mackenzie-Papineau Battalion 31
MacLaine, Shirley 86
MacLennan, John Hugh 166
MacLeod, Alistair 80
MacMaster, Buddy 107, 133
MacMaster, Natalie 107
MacMillan, Scott 17
MacNeil, Rita 77

MacNearney, Eric 56
MacOrdum, Murdock Maxwell 76
Maillard, Abbé Pierre 111, 130
Maliseet peoples 89, 109, 145
Maloney, Denise 61
Manner, David Joseph 83
Manuge, Robert (Bob) 170
maps, provincial 12, 141
Margaree Valley, NS 10
Maritime Labour Herald (newspaper) 154
Massey, Vincent 47
Mauger, Joshua 81
mayflower 66
McCartney, Paul 118
McClung, Nellie L. 127
McCulloch, Thomas 16, 142
McCurdy, Douglas 42
McGregor Mine, explosion 16
McLaughlan, James B. 163
McNab, Catherine Susan Ann 10, 116
Meagher, Blanche Margaret 157
Membertou 61, 157, 160
    Grand Chiefs 95, 126
Melville Island 78, 87, 102, 103
Men of the Deeps 19, 125, 128, 162
Messer, Don 60, 89, 104, 115
Michelin Tire 155, 184
Micmac News (newspaper) 15
Middleton, NS 54
Mi'kma'ki 5, 12, 119
Mi'kmaq 5, 12, 46, 105, 111, 150
    education 38, 58
    Grand Council 69, 73, 119, 152, 183
    history 24, 36, 41, 61, 71, 93, 95, 109,
        124, 126, 130, 135
    Kina'matnewey 38
    people 36, 41, 57, 61, 69, 73, 77, 95,
        119, 134, 157, 160, 169, 184
    raids 89, 93, 149, 181
    Saint Anne 126
    treaty rights 145
Milsom, Scott 107
mines 163, 169
    closure 10
    deaths 16, 24, 33, 35, 65, 74, 90
    explosion 24, 35, 42, 90, 162
    memorializing 52, 89, 128
Minglewood Band 32
Montessori school 121
Moose River Gold Mine 74
Morning Herald (newspaper) 9, 16
Morning Journal (newspaper) 19
Morris, Maria Frances Ann 36
Mosher, A.R. 148
mosques 31, 183
Mount Hanley, NS 82
Mount Saint Vincent University 29, 66
Muise, Molly 95
Murray, Anne 38, 115
museums 8, 17, 23, 24, 27, 44, 52,67, 76, 77,
    115, 118, 125, 136, 140, 137, 177
music
    Academy of 14, 153, 161

Cape Breton 13, 18, 19 43, 128, 133
Celtic 19, 146
festivals 169
folk 76, 146
gospel 17
old-time 60
soul 52
musicians 19, 38, 72, 89, 90, 99, 107, 146

N

National Historic Sites
    Admiralty House 8
    Armoury 185
    Africville 44
    Birchtown 122, 139
    Citadel 143
    Fortress Louisbourg 29
    Grand Pré 113, 133
    Halifax Dockyard 91
    King's College 92
    Port Royal 98
    St. John's Anglican Church (Lunenburg) 162
    St. Paul's Church (Halifax) 138
National Magazine Award 13
Native Communications Society of Nova
    Scotia 15
Navy, Royal 63, 73, 75, 91, 137, 145, 146, 157
Nemon, Oscar 28
New Democratic Party (NDP) 60, 69, 90
New Glasgow, NS 33, 51, 123, 181
New Maritimes (journal) 107
New Ross, NS 118
New Scotland (*see* Scottish)
New Waterford 136, 137
Nile Voyageurs 50
Novadoc (gypsum freighter) 51
Nova Scotia Book of Days 4
Nova Scotia Civil Service Association *see*
    Nova Scotia Government and General
    Employees Union
Nova Scotia College of Art and Design 21,
    37, 139
Nova Scotia Federation of Labour 79
Nova Scotia Government and General
    Employees Union 34, 79
Nova Scotia, founding of 5
Nova Scotia Mass Choir 17, 25
Nova Scotian Institute of Natural Science 21
Novascotian (newspaper) 10, 55, 147
Nowlan, Alden 26

O

Oak Island 132
oil spill 32
Oland's brewery 150
Old Burying Ground (Halifax) 93, 103, 130
Oliver, Rev. William Pearly 98
Olympics 57
OneNS Measurement Collective 55
orchestras 14, 99,
Order of Canada recipients 10, 13, 19, 57,
    73, 77, 85, 98, 107, 120, 133, 136, 137,
    157, 175

Order of Good Cheer (theatre) 168
Order of Nova Scotia, officers 13, 77, 85, 120,
    137, 155, 157, 175
Our Lady of Sorrows Church (Halifax) 137
Owen, William 144

P

Pandora (feminist newspaper) 141
Parsons, Gordon 105
Paul, Daniel 175
Paul, Tom 32
Peace and Friendship Treaty 109
Peggy's Cove, NS 37
Pepperrell, William 68
Perkins, Cato 17
Peters, Thomas 17
Pictou County, NS 118, 145
    mining 16, 35, 90
    people 101, 105, 109, 142
    pollution 21, 149
    railway 63, 99
Pictou Landing First Nation 21, 149, 184
Pier 21 23, 34, 137
Piers, Harry 24
Pittson, Nicholas 'Manny' 104
photography 26, 46
Planters 5, 71, 102, 164
playwrights 13, 15, 78, 81, 123, 146, 178
poets 13, 26, 32, 57, 66, 81, 105, 112, 120,
    144, 146, 184
Point Pleasant Park (Halifax) 56
police 72, 87
politics
    municipal 20, 22, 27, 140
    provincial 21, 31, 34, 69, 73, 75, 84,
        116, 135, 181
pollution *see* environmental pollution
Pony Express 42
Poor Man's Friend Society 40
Pope John Paul II 144
Port de la Baleine, NS 5
    siege of 141
Porter, Gladys (Richardson) 34
Port Hood mine explosion 33
Port Royal, NS 5, 46, 98
Poutrincourt, Jean de Biencourt de 46, 95
poverty 40
Power, Frances 14
Prat, Annie Louise 104
premiers 20, 29, 31, 34, 48, 50, 62, 73, 75, 84,
    115, 118, 142, 161, 164, 170, 172, 184
Presbyterian churches 116
Preston, NS 120
Prince Edward 112
Progressive Conservatives 34, 50, 73, 101, 164
prohibition 19, 51, 133
Province House (Halifax) 151, 156, 166, 175
Pugwash, NS 149, 184
Purcell, Joseph 78

Q

Queen Elizabeth II 57, 85, 124, 165
Queen Hotel fire (Halifax) 48

Queen Victoria 20, 62, 66, 110, 114, 135

R
racial segregation 33, 55
Raddall, Thomas H. 167
radio
    broadcasts 35, 74, 90, 100, 141
    stations 60, 90, 92, 104
    see also CHNS
railway 144, 146
    Canadian National 52, 122
    Intercolonial 15, 16, 63, 94, 122, 129
    Nova Scotia 63, 99, 101, 106, 128, 133, 183
    streetcar 37, 106
Raines, Robert 14
Rankin Family 18
Ramsey, George 158
RCMP 72
Red Cross 57, 80, 91
refugees 23, 31, 83, 86, 87, 91
Regan, Geoff 174
Richardson, Evelyn 102
Rinpoche, Chögyam Trungpa 66
riots, VE Day 88, 98
Ritchie, Charles S.A. 104, 140
Ritchie, Eliza 140
Ritchie, John W. 136, 140
Rogers, Stan 173
Roman Catholicism 10, 65, 85, 126, 131
Rose, Clifford, 51
Royal Acadian School 16
Royal Canadian Regiment 19
Royal Charter, colonization 5
Royal Nova Scotia Historical Society 9, 24
Royal William (steamship) 133
rum
    Fortress Louisbourg 45
    running 19, 59
    see also prohibition

S
Sackville, NS 105
sailing vessels 8, 59, 133, 145, 148, 152, 154, 157, 160
Salter Street Films 36
Saunders, Margaret M. 93
Scottish, Highland 5, 51, 124, 132, 145, 152
Scottish 5, 81, 119, 122, 132, 145, 173
    tartan 51
Sealy, Joe 52
Seaview United Baptist Church (Africville) 44
Second World War 4, 25, 75, 77, 119, 145, 182
    Pier 21 23
Shelburne 102, 139
shipwrecks 64, 80, 88, 89, 154, 155, 166, 183
Shubenacadie, NS 69
    river 81, 144
Sikh Society, Maritime 82
Silver Dart (airplane) 42
Sinclair, Alexander MacLean 48
Singalong Jubilee 60, 85, 89, 104, 115, 170
slavery 5, 17, 81, 120
Slocum, Joshua 82

Smith, Noel Abraham 'Abe' 119
Snow, Hank, 39, 90
Sobey, Frank 181
South Bar, NS 13
Spanish
    Civil War 31
    Influenza 102
Sparks, Corrine 130
Spatz, Jim 34
Spatz Theatre 46
Spring Garden Memorial Library 28
Springhill, NS 38, 42, 129, 158, 162, 183
Stadacona, Canadian Forces 8
Stanfield, Robert 34, 50, 73, 164
Stead, Bob 20
Stellarton, NS 24, 182, 183
St. Francis Xavier University 48, 51, 96, 128
St. John's Church (Lunenburg) 162
St. Mary's University 50, 66, 155
St. Peter's Nova Scotia 26
streetcars 37
St. Roch (schooner) 154
Supreme Court, provincial 33, 49
Sydney, NS 30, 47, 59, 85, 86, 101, 123
    Steel Corporation 30, 154
Symphony Nova Scotia 17, 99

T
telephone
    company mergers 80
    demonstration 20
    dial 40
temperance 28, 35, 51, 91
theatres 25, 33, 39, 46, 47, 59, 161, 162, 168, 172
Thistle Penny 8
Titanic 76, 79
Trailer Park Boys 177
Treaty of Utrecht 63
Trotsky, Leon 78
Truro, NS 15
Tupper, Charles 84, 115, 161
Tynes, Maxine 144

U
UNESCO
    Biosphere Reserves 113
    Heritage Sites 113, 116, 176
Uniacke, James Boyle 20, 31, 122, 170
Uniacke, Richard John 170
Unionist and Halifax Journal 19
Union of Nova Scotia Indians 15, 160, 183
unions, recognition of 34

V
Vaughn, Garth 138
Vietnamese Association of Nova Scotia 16
Vimy Ridge, Battle of 70
Vogue Theatre (Sydney) 47
Voice of Women 171

W
Wagner, Frances 165
Wallis, William Parry 73

Walters, Angus J. 61, 130
War of 1812 83, 87, 100
War of Independence, American 5
Waverley, NS 89
Weekly Chronicle (newspaper) 10
Welsford-Parker Memorial (Halifax) 121
Wentworth, John 58, 69, 71, 143
Westin Nova Scotian Hotel 110
West Pubnico, NS 35
Westray mining disaster 90, 174
White Point, NS 39
White, Portia 108, 110
White, William A. 108
Whycocomagh, NS 57
Wilde, Oscar 153
Wilkson, Moses 'Daddy' 17
Williams, Sinclair 87
Williams, William Fenwick 135
Wilson, Budge 85
Windsor, NS 33, 92, 100, 140
    Avon River 21, 58, 182
    hockey 96, 138
    railway 63, 101, 128, 133
wine making 108
Wisdom, Jane Barnes 105
Wolfe, James 90, 97, 124
Wolfville, NS 14, 20, 27, 86, 104, 120, 172
women
    awards to 52, 57, 91
    Halifax history 46, 79, 127, 137, 141, 165
    Royal Commission on the Status of 39
    suffrage 82, 140
Woods, David 81
Wright, George Henry 79

Y
Yarmouth, NS 105, 128
    ships 8, 133, 166, 181
YMCA 35

Z
Zwicker, Marguerite 147